OLD SANTA FE

A Brief Review of History 1536–1912

East San Francisco Street, Santa Fe, NM ca. 1866
(Courtesy Museum of New Mexico, Neg.#31339)

OLD SANTA FE

A Brief Review of History 1536–1912

JAMES J. RACITI

SANTA FE

On the cover:
Deposition on a Fraudulent Land Grant Case
(Courtesy State Library of New Mexico)

Sunstone books may be purchased for educational, business, or sales promotional use.
For information please write: Special Markets Department, Sunstone Press, P.O. Box 2321, Santa Fe, New Mexico 87504-2321.

Library of Congress Cataloging-in-Publication Data:

Raciti, James J., 1933–
    Old Santa Fe: a brief review of history, 1536–1912 / by James J. Raciti
        p. cm.
    ISBN: 0-86534-393-4 (softcover)
    1.Santa Fe (N.M.)—History.   I. Title.
    F804.S257 R327 2003
    978.9'56—dc21   2003010370

Published in

SUNSTONE PRESS
POST OFFICE BOX 2321
SANTA FE, NM 87504-2321 / USA
(505) 988-4418 / *ORDERS ONLY* (800) 243-5644
FAX (505) 988-1025
WWW.SUNSTONEPRESS.COM

Contents

Acknowledgements

I would like to thank the Publisher of Sunstone Press, Jim Smith for his excellent ideas, his timely advice and his encouragement for this project.

I would also like to thank the New Mexico State Librarian, Ben Wakashige and his staff for their guidance and patience as I plowed through their archives and special collections for my research. Thanks also to Arthur Olivas of the Palace of the Governors Archives for his assistance in selecting historical photos and drawings. A special thanks to Tom Chavez and his staff for pertinent historical background on the museum and monuments.

Lastly, I'd like to thank my wife, Maryhelen for her good counsel, her assiduous reading of the manuscript and her excellent suggestions.

Santa Fe County Courthouse after fire of February 8, 1909
(Courtesy Museum of New Mexico, Neg.#105580), Photo by Anna L. Hase

Chronology

1536: Cabeza de Vaca and party cross the Southwest

1540: Coronado explores Gulf of California to Kansas

1598: Juan de Oñate founds San Juan de los Caballeros

1610: Governor Pedro de Peralta establishes capital at Santa Fe
Construction begins on Palace of the Governors

1680: Unified Pueblo Revolt under Popé

1693: Don Diego de Vargas colonizes Santa Fe for Spain

1706: Albuquerque founded

1743: French trappers reach Santa Fe and start trade with Spanish

1786: Governor Anza makes peace with Comanches

1807: Zebulon Pike leads first Anglo-American expedition to area

1821: Signing of Treaty of Cordova; Independence from Spain; Santa Fe
Trail opens to international trade

1837: Chimayo Revolt against taxation; Killing of Governor Perez

1841: Texas invades New Mexico to extend its border

1846: Mexican-American War; Kearny takes New Mexico

1847: Taos Revolt against military; Governor Bent killed

1848: Treaty of Guadalupe Hidalgo ends Mexican-American War

1850: New Mexico becomes US territory; Statehood denied

1851: Reverend Jean Baptiste Lamy arrives in Santa Fe

1854: Gadsden Purchase from Mexico; New Mexico augments size

1861: Formation of Colorado Territory to include San Luis Valley; Texas Confederates invade New Mexico

1862: Battles of Glorieta Pass; Confederates leave New Mexico; Apaches and Navajos relocated to Bosque Redondo

1863: New Mexico partitioned to create Arizona Territory

1864: Colonel Kit Carson makes war on Navajos at Canyon de Chelly

1878: Railroad arrives in New Mexico but bypasses Santa Fe; Lincoln County War erupts in southeast New Mexico; Lew Wallace appointed territorial governor

1880: Adolph Bandelier begins survey of archaeological ruins; Spur railroad line to Santa Fe

1881: Billy the Kid shot by Sheriff Pat Garrett at Fort Sumner

1886: Geronimo's surrender ends Apache wars in Southwest

1888: Archbishop Lamy dies

1889: President Harrison appoints L. Bradley Prince governor

1891: Free public education law passed by legislature

1897: President McKinley appoints M.A. Otero governor

1912: New Mexico obtains Statehood

Preface

This book was prepared with various readers in mind. It is first for those local readers who want a handy and easy-to-read review of the historical events that have shaped this wonderful "City Different." Then there are those visitors to Santa Fe who want to identify names, styles and locations as they walk around the city, reliving the past. Readers, who have little background in history, at whatever age, may also find this little book informative and interesting and it may entice them to read more deeply into some of the lesser-known historical facts. This book makes no attempt at an erudite study of Santa Fe or the Southwest. We can safely say that no significant new ground has been broken.

As the title suggests, this book is about Santa Fe. The city that we have grown to love as a great center for the arts, for theater, music and for its impressive ancient buildings did not just happen as if touched by a magic wand. Santa Fe did not just burst upon the scene fully grown and formed. Rather, it is the result of painstaking effort on the part of thousands of people be they native Pueblo Indians who cultivated the soil and built their communities or the Spanish settlers who introduced a different way of life. Therefore, it is Santa Fe that we contemplate, first as a Spanish province, then as a province of Mexico, later as a territory of the United States and finally as the forty-seventh State of the Union. We go beyond the city limits to include all those incredible places and people that played a part in the creation of this city. Santa Fe was not the first capital of New Mexico but it became so on its second try. The book begins with the early natives of the land, then of Cabeza de Vaca and Esteban, the Moor, Coronado and Oñate. This gives a background to understanding the difficulties encountered by both the Spanish settlers and the native Indians. We have selected to speak of four centuries but have not gone very far into the twentieth. This is an arbitrary choice and does not mean that some very significant events of that century, or our present one, are not worthy of comment. In addition to recounting the past, we have put some emphasis on the religious and educational motivation in order to show the struggling development of the human condition. Wars were the result of conflicting ideals. They were fought in defense of what were considered basic rights. Wars were also fought to propagate beliefs that were held, at the time, to be absolute truths.

This book is not only about great leaders but also about bad ones. It's about those who supported their superiors with strength and dignity, often giving their lives in sacrifice. And it's also about those subordinates who were determined to undermine their leaders. For example, much of Coronado's failure came about because he trusted those close to him who secretly wanted to see him fail. Peralta's excellent work as a builder and pioneer was degraded by the excessive pride and arrogance of a church official determined to bring the Governor down. It was a much lesser man, consumed by jealousy and willing to resort to calumny that sullied the career of de Vargas and caused him to be imprisoned.

But through glory and misery, through success and failure, Santa Fe has survived. Its history is not without brutality and intrigue, murder and betrayal and several mass atrocities. Its history is a struggle to find peace, security and enlightenment. From a finely textured past to a richly varied present, Santa Fe has become for its visitors a must-see destination, a frequent pilgrimage or a second home.

1

The Land

In the Jemez Mountains, west of the city of Santa Fe, there is a wide valley called "Valle Grande." The valley was created by an ancient volcano, which erupted some 1.2 million years ago with a force, it has been estimated, at about 300 times that of Washington's Mt. Saint Helen, and deposited debris as far as Louisiana and Kansas. In places, the ash was more than 1000 feet thick. It was in this area that the first natives settled after making their way south from Chaco Canyon and Mesa Verde.

The city of Santa Fe is the oldest capital in the United States. It is second only to St. Augustine, Florida as the oldest city in the country. These facts are true if we do not count the city dwellers of the Anasazi. The oldest pueblo in New Mexico is Acoma which has been inhabited continuously since around 1075 A.D.

Santa Fe is situated at 7,000 feet of altitude, in the north central part of the state. It has been called the Land of *Poco Tiempo*, which can mean "little time" or "time means little." The city's full name is: "The Royal City of the Holy Faith of San Francisco d'Assisi."

The State of New Mexico covers 121,666 square miles making it the fifth largest state in the Union. Before the Arizona territory was sectioned away, New Mexico bordered California. The state is an almost perfect rectangle; it measures 390 miles north to south and 350 miles east to west.

At the elevation of Santa Fe, snow falls in winter but melts quickly. There is an abundance of piñon and juniper trees. Above 8,000 feet one finds the ponderosa pine, which gives way to the aspen at higher altitudes. Wildlife around the Santa Fe area includes foxes, skunks, porcupines and sometimes larger animals like antelope, bighorn sheep and even bears. The ubiquitous coyote can be found in many of the neighborhoods of the city.

The major rivers of New Mexico are the Rio Grande, Pecos, Canadian, San Juan and Gila. Water has always played an important role in the development of the state. The inhabitants prior to 1900 (when they learned to use ground water) had to rely only on water sources from the rivers.

The mean annual temperature for the state is about 53 degrees Fahrenheit but can vary as much as 26 degrees at different locations. Precipitation is an important factor in the climate. Here is where New Mexico is deficient. The annual average precipitation is only 15 inches, with the mountains and the eastern part of the state having more rain and snow.

The apparent deficiencies for the early settlers were the following: lack of rainfall, extreme isolation, lack of navigable rivers, lack of timber in much of the province and lack of minerals. Of the above, only isolation and lack of minerals has changed. The early Spaniards had little knowledge of geography and assumed that the land of New Mexico was only a short day's overland journey from the coast of Florida. Distances were understood in terms of the distances they knew in Spain. Lack of water plagued the early natives and settlers; this continues to be a problem today. Centuries of Moorish occupation in Spain taught the Spaniards the importance of gathering water in cisterns below their houses. The early Spaniards in New Mexico carried this important information with them but over the centuries it became lost or forgotten. Much of the rainfall we receive today runs off and is gone and each year we remain badly prepared for the many months of drought. Because of sediment and silt, our storage capacities continue to decrease. We have become demanding and voracious in our need for water, unlike the early Americans who made judicious use of this precious resource.

14

2

Early Americans

Evidence exists that humans lived in the Sandia area of New Mexico as early as 25,000 years before Christ. Basic tools and weapons of hunt were found near Clovis, New Mexico dating from 10,000 to 9,000 years before the Christian era.

We are not certain of the origins of the people who populated the land we now call New Mexico. Some believe they came from Asia over what is popularly known as the ice bridge that joined Russia to Alaska, following the migrating herds. It was believed that these people migrated south over the plains searching for a more agreeable climate. Others believed they came from the south, land now known as Central America searching for richer soil for their crops. What we do know for certain is that these people, whatever their name or origin, lived on the land the Spaniards began to occupy as early as the 1500s. Of the many names they have been called such as "Our People," "Our Nation" etc., the name that stands out is the "Anasazi People." Curiously enough, this was not a name they gave to themselves but rather a term in the Navajo language, meaning enemy of our ancestors and later simply "ancient people."

An arbitrary but useful classification of the American Indian may be made as follows: 1) by the language they speak; 2) by their physical or anatomical characteristics; and 3) by the way they live. Because the Pueblo Indians preferred to build communities, till the land and remain in one place for long periods of time, they differed from the Plains Indians. The Plains Indians constituted for a much longer time than we realized, the most effective barrier set up by any American Native population against the European invaders. Even after the Spaniards settled parts of the Southwest, travelers would take great pains, going hundreds of miles out of their way to avoid crossing the dangerous plains.

Anasazi

Extending east from the Arizona border into New Mexico as far as Los Alamos and extending south from the Colorado border into New Mexico as far as Albuquerque is the land of the Anasazi. Evidence of their presence goes back to about 5,000 years before the Christian era. These people could build and sustain fire, gather seeds, nuts and fruit. Building permanent dwellings allowed them to cultivate the soil near their villages. Their crops were corn, squash and beans. They learned the art of saving what they could not eat immediately in woven containers. Later they learned how to make pottery for carrying and preserving their water. It is relatively easy to date the accomplishments of these people. We are unable, however, to know with certainty their reasons for abandoning these settlements. It could have been that the game they relied on was depleted or the water supply had run out.

Bandelier National Monument

This site is named after Adolph Bandelier, a Swiss ethnologist. It is in the heart of the Frijoles Canyon. Here, several centuries before the arrival of the white man, the Anasazi people settled. It is believed that the drought of the late 13th century forced them to seek a water supply on the banks of the upper Rio Grande Valley. On the Pararito Plateau they constructed intricate dwellings in the soft volcanic ash on the sides of the canyon. The Anasazi were referred to as "Pueblo Indians" by the Spaniards because they built their dwellings in the form of villages and cultivated their crops, quite different from the

16

nomad tribes who contructed no permanent dwellings. Entering these dwellings required considerable climbing, which only primates can do, thus protecting themselves from the dangerous carnivores. Evidence remained long after the disappearance of these people that they chipped stones into weapons of hunt; they preserved food supplies in baskets they made for this purpose, and they protected their feet by wearing leather coverings. These Pueblo Indians were farmers, hunters and gatherers and they enjoyed a communal life rich in spiritual values. Bandelier wanted to study these interesting people so he lived in a kiva, examined hundreds of ruins and wrote numerous scientific papers. He published a fictionalized account of the inhabitants of Frijoles Canyon called *The Delight Makers* in 1890.

Corn Dance, Cochiti Pueblo, July 14, 1888 (Courtesy Museum of New Mexico, Neg .#117651)
Photo by Charles F. Lummis

The Apaches

The Apaches, a nomadic tribe, earned for themselves the reputation for being particularly savage in their raids of the Pueblo Indians and the Spanish settlers in the Southwest. The Apaches originally migrated to the Southwest from northwestern Canada and Alaska, where Athabascan tribes, speaking closely related languages, still live today.

Unlike the Pueblo Indians, the Apaches grew no crops and built no permanent dwellings. The Apaches had names, which described their main occupations. For example, the Mescalero Apaches were so named because they were makers of mescal. They took this liquid from that desert plant of the agave family and used it as a beverage and as food.

The Jicarilla Apaches were basket makers—sometimes described as indolent and unwilling to meet confrontation. They were driven from their homeland by the war-like Comanches and retreated into the mountains of Northern New Mexico. After many years of war and the defeat of their great leader Geronimo, the Apaches were confined to reservations, putting an end to their aggressive way of life.

The Comanches

As early as 1694, when the Spaniards installed a new Friar in Pecos and this community began to thrive as a trading post, the Comanches made their appearance. The annual fair in Pecos had become an important meeting place for various Indian tribes and Spaniards alike. The Comanches who had migrated into New Mexico from the basin and range country of the Rockies put an end to the lucrative trade at Pecos. The Jicarilla Apaches fled from the warring Comanches and the trade at Pecos fell off. Most of the raids on the Pueblo Indians were to acquire horses. During one such raid on the Pecos Indians, the Comanches encountered Spanish troops from Santa

Fe and fought a fierce battle with them. That day nine soldiers were killed—a great loss for the Spaniards.

The Pecos Indians, typical of the Pueblo People, were an easy target of the marauding Comanches who would wait in hiding and pounce on their unsuspecting prey, steal what they could, inflict harm and often death, then disappear. So angered and afraid were the Pecos that they gave up trying to cultivate the unprotected land along the Pecos River. In 1779, the new and very astute governor of New Mexico, Juan Bautista de Anza defeated the Comanches in a battle in what is today Colorado. In this battle, the Spaniards killed the Comanche Chief Green Horn. Anza became a man the Comanches could surrender to without loss of honor. In 1786, Governor Anza made a permanent peace with the Comanches.

The Navajos

The Navajos were an important sub-group of the Apaches that dominated western New Mexico for centuries. They were considered Athapascans because of their linguistic origins. The Athapascans traveled south originally from Alaska and northern Canada and first encountered the Anasazi in The Four Corners area. The Navajo tribe developed a culture of its own. It has been long considered that the Athapascans who adopted the Pueblo ways became Navajos. Those who preferred to continue the wild life of raiding, stealing and killing became the true Apaches. Before the arrival of the Spaniards, there was an extensive trade among the various tribes. Hides, dried meat and tallow were exchanged for maize and cotton blankets of the more sedentary Indians.

With the arrival of the Spaniards, a new element was introduced—the desire to impose a religion and a way of life on others. The mind of the Navajo Indian, politically naïve and untutored in European Catholicism, could not grasp the subtleties of the messages brought by the Spanish friars. The freedom-loving Navajos were at constant odds with the Spaniards. While accepting some of the habits of the Pueblo Indians, the Navajos preferred their nomad existence, continued to raid and were even guilty of slaving against their enemy tribes. They were often just as brutal as the Spaniards.

Preston writes: "At one point, a group of Navajos came into Taos with some Pawnee boys captured on the plains. When they found the boys couldn't be sold, they decapitated them and left."

The dwellings of the Navajos were the hogans built of wood and stone and covered with earth. They looked like beehives and still can be seen dotting the landscape of western New Mexico. Of all the nomadic people, they have perhaps attained the highest degree of civilization. Much later it was the Navajos who encouraged the Pueblo Indians to revolt against the Spaniards in 1680 and collaborated with them in the uprising.

Native Americans still populate New Mexico and the Southwest. Some would argue that the term "Native American" is inappropriate. The truth of the matter is that they were the owners of the land before the arrival of the foreigners. The white man has learned from them and they have learned, in turn, from him. It is a pity that some of their notable traits such as the respect for the land and the rivers have not been fully accepted by the more "civilized" populations. How civilized it is to leave no trace of your passing—like an arrow through the air or the fish through water!

Although the horse existed in North America (we know this from skeletal remains) and probably came over the ice bridge from Asia, the people of the Southwest did not know of it until the arrival of Coronado in 1540. Fossil remains indicate that horses roamed both North and South America but disappeared long before the 1400s. We know what the arrival of the horse meant to the Plains Indians. So important was the horse to the Plains Indians that the anthropologists have named the period from 1540-1880s—the "Horse-Culture" Period. As the Pueblo Indians learned the usefulness of this extraordinary animal, they began to raise large herds and started selling and trading them to other Indians such as the Kiowas and Comanches. When the Apaches, along with the other nomad tribes, acquired this exceptional animal, the danger to settled Indian populations and to the white man became acute.

3

Early Spaniards

Reviewing history is much like eating a rice dish: one can start almost anywhere. To trace the influence of Spain in the "New World," we should look first at the exploration by Christopher Columbus of the Americas under the combined houses of Aragon and Castila. In the wake of Columbus' discovery, the Spanish invaded, explored and conquered much of the Western Hemisphere. When the Spaniards arrived in Mexico in 1492, the population of Mexico was about 25 million. That population dropped to 6 million in 1548 and by the end of the century was only 1,350,000 of whom one hundred thousand were Spaniards. These figures speak for the ruthlessness of the invaders in the New World and their propensity to spread fatal diseases among the natives. In battle, the superiority of the Spaniards was incontestable. Their weapons included steel swords and explosives. They presented a formidable sight in their gleaming armor astride animals unknown to the natives—horses. These conquerors believed that they had been given a mission by God to take dominion over all the infidels. Cynics may say that under the guise of bringing Christianity to the natives, the invaders were only after gold and silver.

Cabeza de Vaca

Under Cortes in 1521, the thirst for precious metals reached a feverish level. In 1530, Alvar Nunez Cabeza de Vaca reported after his travels throughout the Southwest seeing cities of gold. Perhaps what he saw were huts built of mud and straw, which glimmered in the sunlight. Cabeza de Vaca told of his adventures, which began in 1527 when he and six hundred men left Spain in five vessels and landed near Tampa Bay in western Florida. The expedition had only one goal—the seeking of gold. The Spaniards found little to eat and were poorly prepared for an extended search. The men became greatly weakened, suffering from malaria. All they could find to eat were oysters. In desperation, they killed and ate their horses. Believing that Mexico was immediately adjacent to Florida, they traveled along the Gulf Coast. In a small boat, Cabeza de Vaca and his men drifted aimlessly for days until they came ashore on a barrier island, now believed to be Galveston Island.

The writings of Cabeza de Vaca tell of a black Moorish slave named Esteban one of the few survivors with himself to endure more than a year of captivity among a local tribe of Indians. Upon relating to the Spanish viceroy in Mexico the years of wandering through the Southwest, much of the time with his companion Esteban, Cabeza de Vaca particularly excited the viceroy's interest with the mention of great cities to the north and the elaborately dressed women wearing jewelry. The viceroy asked him to go back to lead a reconnaissance party but Cabeza de Vaca declined. The African, Esteban, however, agreed.

In 1538, the Spanish viceroy in Mexico, Antonio Mendoza, made a Franciscan priest, Marcos de Niza, the leader in a reconnaissance of the lands north of Mexico. Marcos de Niza immediately put Esteban in charge of an advanced party of Aztecs. Esteban had no sooner entered the first of the Seven Cities than he and almost all of his men were slain by arrows. Within a year, the priest returned to Mexico City claiming to have seen a large city that the Zuni Indians called Cibola. This city was supposed to be only one of seven cities of gold. Friar Marcos de Niza wrote the following upon seeing Cibola from a distance:

"Judging by what I could see from the height where I had placed myself to observe it, the settlement is larger than the City of Mexico

...It appears that this land is the best and largest of all those that have been discovered."

Francisco Vazquez de Coronado

Marcos de Niza's reports ignited an even greater lust for gold. Viceroy Mendoza was so impressed he wanted to lead an expedition himself—perhaps to rival De Soto's successes in Florida. Instead, he commissioned a young nobleman by the name of Francisco Vazquez de Coronado—just thirty years old. In February of 1540, Coronado departed the town of Compostela with about three hundred soldiers, a few Franciscans, more than a thousand Indian slaves and more than fifteen hundred horses and pack animals.

In a letter to the King of Spain, to give some idea of their short trips around the villages, Coronado wrote: ". . . with only thirty horsemen whom I took for my escort, I traveled forty-two days, living all this while solely on the flesh of the bulls and cows which we killed and going many days without water, and cooking the food with cow dung, because there is not any kind of wood in all these plains."
Establishing a base among the Pueblo villages along the Rio Grande, Coronado explored parts of Arizona, New Mexico, Texas, Oklahoma and Kansas. Why did he venture into the plains? A man called the "Turk," whose reasons are unclear, had lied to him about the existence of the cities of gold. Perhaps it was to lose the Spaniards in the wilderness where there was insufficient food and little water. Jaramillo (recorder of the journey) wrote: "We understood, however, that he (the Turk) was leading us away from the route we ought to follow . . . so we would eat up all the food . . . and become weak."

It was not until springtime of 1542 that Coronado made his way back to Mexico, having failed in his mission of procuring gold for his king. Coronado realized that Friar Marcos had lied about the gold. With each step of this journey, he had been assured, by those closest to him, that the cities of gold were just over the horizon. The Spaniards garroted the Turk for his treachery and left him where he fell. The great riches of Mexico and Peru had not materialized in this barren country.

History bears out that, although Coronado's men were greatly outnumbered, they inflicted heavy damage on the Pueblo Indians whenever these native people refused to do the bidding of the invaders. Along with the devastation from their firearms, Coronado's soldiers brought disease to these native people. A protégé of Mendoza, Coronado wanted more than monetary wealth for himself, he wanted to be hailed as a great conqueror, a hero for the Spanish people. However, it was thanks to the efforts of Coronado and his men that new maps were drawn of the regions, which greatly assisted those who followed him. Of the Europeans, it was he who learned first that California was not an island; it was he who first saw the Rocky Mountains and ventured into the Great Plains.

For an entire generation, no further expeditions were made into New Mexico. Fray Agustin Rodriquez led a group of missionaries into New Mexico in 1581 but they were all killed. In 1590, Gaspar Castaño led an unauthorized expedition into New Mexico but was chased by the Spanish army and imprisoned. A street in historic Santa Fe is named after him—Don Gaspar.

4

Religion & Myth in the 17th Century

One can easily understand but not so easily condone the arrogance of the conquering Spaniards in matters of religion. Had they not been taught that the Holy Catholic Church was the true Church and all other religions were false and evil? Accompanying the soldiers were always men of the cloth—Franciscan friars who maintained that these natives were nothing but beasts because they had not had the sacrament of baptism. It was the duty of the Church to bring the blessings of Christianity to these lost souls.

It would take centuries of enlightenment to understand that praying in a dance is no different than praying on one's knees; that seeking help from the earth mother was no different than praying to the Virgin. It would take centuries of enlightenment to want to understand and value the religious beliefs of the natives.

The time of the Spanish conquest of the Americas was not a time of enlightenment, as we know it. Those who would not submit to the holy sacraments were put to death. If the Franciscan friars could have understood the Indians, they would have learned that the reverence they held for animals was respect for what that animal could teach. The rattlesnake, for example, could teach the native how to move quietly through the grass and strike its prey without being heard. The power of the bird was that it could soar high above the canyons in minutes while it took man hours and perhaps days to cover the same distance. It was to the bird that they asked help to attain these powers. The Spaniard viewed the Indian's frank and totally unconscious nudity and his phallic worship to be depraved. One can remember that in pre-Christian Pompeii, the concern with fertility led the inhabitants to use the phallic as a token of strength. Much of what we marvel at today in Pompeii was covered up by volcanic ash for centuries and discovered only at a time when we, through understanding, could view such art with objective interest.

Because the Franciscans would not understand, the natives accepted the dictates of the Catholic Church but went underground and kept their own beliefs in secret. The kiva was a place of reflection and prayer, deep within the earth away from critical eyes. The kivas were dug below the earth and were circular in shape. The Spaniards who saw them thought they were used for cooking and named them "estufas" or stoves. It was later that they learned that this was a holy place where the elders of the community gathered to seek help in their prayers for decisions they were contemplating.

Through the development of science, the white man learned what god was not. Unlike the Greeks and Romans, he no longer worshiped the sea, the sun or the wind. The Indian, however, had a complete and personal relationship with nature and manifested his religious beliefs through prayers, dances and songs. He who seemed to be able to interpret the will of the gods was the Shaman. These men had a special relationship with the gods, wore distinctive outerwear, feathers and masks to emphasize their importance. Where confusion existed, they brought clarity; they were the decision makers. Who, indeed, would question the man so close to the gods? They were able by some mystic power within themselves to create "good" medicine and dispel "bad" medicine.

Symbolism plays an important part in all religions. Christians have the Cross, a symbol of the sacrificing of life and its resurrection. Catholics take the Host into their mouths at Holy Communion symbolic of eating the body of Christ. The Shaman wears the mask of the deity he is communicating with to personify this deity. The Catholic uses the Rosary Beads in prayer; the native uses the Pahos, or prayer stick, often made up of eagle feathers to symbolize that, as the eagle soars into the eye of the sun, so may his prayers ascend to the Divine Ones.

Witchcraft was universal among the Indian tribes and superstition a prime factor in their lives. Whatever the untutored mind did not understand became associated with some occult power. Young mothers were especially vulnerable. Witches were known to be baby snatchers. Mothers were especially solicitous of their infants. They would cover their children's heads and faces whenever they came into the presence of a witch. The Indians would be careful not to be ostentatious of ownership of any beautiful string of beads or brightly colored blanket for fear that they might cause a witch to be jealous of them. Deformity was always the result of a curse. If a dead cat were to be thrown near a person, that person would be seized with paralysis. Witches thrived in darkness and shadows. They could assume the shape of animals and enter the very smallest spaces. They could travel great distances in the blink of an eye.

Inflicting pain upon ones own body is not strictly a peculiarity of early Christians imitating the passion of Jesus Christ. The ancient Egyptians whipped themselves in honor of Isis. Likewise evidence of self-flagellation was witnessed in Sparta. Although the Order of *Los Hermanos Penitentes* was founded in Spain over 300 years ago, in direct disobedience of the papal bull, which prohibited this activity, the Spanish conquistadors upon arriving in New Mexico found traces of a similar custom. Lummis writes: "It is interesting to note that tribal penance, vicariously done, has been a custom among Pueblo Indians from time immemorial, and still is observed. Twice a year, in each of the nineteen now-inhabited pueblos, a penitential fast of four days is kept . . . In Isleta six men and six women are selected to expiate for the sins of the whole pueblo."

All the Pueblo tribes had their professional penitents. Some inflicted pain on themselves with the thorns of the cactus. It was the Mexicans in the Southwest, however, who bought this activity to levels that brought condemnation. They would whip themselves with iron nails, carry wooden crosses to exhaustion and allow themselves to be crucified. It may not be overstated to say that these penitents, by inflicting great pain on themselves and then denying the existence of this pain, were able to reach high levels of spiritual bliss.

Taboos play a role in many religions. Jews, for example, will not mix milk dishes with meat dishes. Catholics, for centuries, would not eat meat on Fridays or have food in their stomachs when they took Holy Communion. Many taboos have their origin in sensible customs—do not eat in a stranger's house, do not fall asleep in an unfamiliar place. Among the Zunis of New Mexico, there are those who may never eat the flesh of a badger, bear or coyote. To the Navajos, fish, ducks, snakes and rabbits are taboo.

The relative power of the gods plays an important role. In prayer, one cannot approach an all-powerful god directly but only through the good graces of a less powerful god. Catholics pray to their favorite saints to intercede with the Virgin for help with their prayers. When the Pueblo Indians witnessed the arrival of the Spanish soldiers and priests along the Camino Real and saw above them the dark clouds of rain, they believed that the gods of these people had to be more powerful than their own gods. For hadn't the Indians been praying for rain during many months of drought with no success while these strangers brought the rain with them?

5

Don Juan de Oñate

Personal Ambition

By 1595, the disappointments of Viceroy Mendoza and Coronado may have been forgotten. A new viceroy for the crown—Luis de Velasco signed a contract with a wealthy man for the occupation and colonization of the land that would be called "New Mexico." This was Don Juan de Oñate. He was persistent in his urgings and a good friend of the viceroy but perhaps not the best person for this task. Unlike his predecessors who traveled north from Mexico City to pillage whatever wealth they could, Oñate was a businessman, made wealthy from the silver mining in Zacatecas. He was married to Isabel de Tolosa Cortes Moctezuma, the granddaughter of Hernan Cortez and the great granddaughter of Moctezuma. He would bear the cost of the expedition and by contract would receive the title of governor and enjoy a share of the profits this new kingdom would produce. He would be paid a salary of 6,000 ducats a year and have an unlimited power, reporting only to the Council of the Indies in Spain. Camping along the banks of the Rio Concho in what is now northern Mexico, Oñate waited for the political wrangling to cease so that he could have permission to head north. All the time, he spent large sums of his own money to maintain the men in arms and the other colonists. Finally in 1598, he set forth, with about 130 soldier-settlers, their wives, children and servants and eight priests, traveling in eighty-five wagons. This brought the total number of people to about 500. With great difficulty, the caravan crossed the arid Mexican desert. Food was scarce and water was difficult to find. One expeditionary member, poet-soldier Gaspar Perez de Villagra wrote: "Two of the thirst-crazed horses" when they finally reached the banks of the Rio Grande, "drank so much that their bellies burst open."

After passing the spot that was later named "El Paso", Oñate proclaimed Spanish dominion over the new land and all its inhabitants, "from the leaves of the trees in the forests to the stones and sands of the river."

Oñate's party traveled north over the dry stretch where the Rio Grande disappeared underground and was given food and drink in a village, which, in gratitude, he named Socorro, meaning "help" in Spanish. Again Perez de Villagra wrote: "... the light party arrived at the pueblo of Teypana on June 14, 1598 where they received a most gracious welcome. Chief Letoc was not only generous with his corn, but he also provided the Spaniards with valuable information about the land and the people ahead."

This caravan made up of about eighty-five wagons, extended several miles long with its livestock numbering in the thousands.

North of present-day Santa Fe, near what is now the town of Espanola, Oñate made his headquarters in the Tewa Pueblo of San Juan, chasing the natives from their lodgings. Oñate ordered the construction of St. Gabriel, New Mexico's first capital.

Although the main purpose for establishing a governor for New Mexico was the pacification and Christianization of the Indians, Oñate had a hidden agenda of seeking out any silver mines he could find. He had brought along heavy mining tools and supplies for that purpose. It can be disputed that Oñate had the best interests of New Spain and the King of Spain at heart. He may have had good intentions of showing the natives kindness but it is difficult for us to understand fully the mentality of the armed men who invaded New Mexico. To enter a land where tribes of people lived, hunted and tilled the earth and to claim everything in view for the Spanish Crown is a bit difficult for us to accept. Not only did the Spaniards claim the land but they also forced the natives to feed their armies and kneel to an unknown god. The 46 year-old Oñate may have lacked maturity to be a benevolent statesman. Perhaps he was not more brutal or greedy than his predecessors but he has been perceived as such.

Because of his preoccupation with finding silver mines and his need for approval from the viceroy, Oñate became an absent leader, traveling as far as the Gulf of California and into present-day Kansas. He all but ignored the hardships of the settlers, many of whom deserted the settlement and returned to Mexico. During these first years, many letters of complaint were sent to the viceroy, which were balanced by the optimism Oñate displayed in his own reports of impending success of finding riches.

Cruel Retaliation

Perhaps one of the most salient episodes, which comes down to us today, is that of the destruction of Acoma, west of present-day Albuquerque. On top of a 400-foot high mesa, protected on all sides by steep cliffs, the Pueblo of Acoma stood since about 1075. The Acoma warriors were greatly feared by the surrounding pueblos. When Juan de Oñate went to Acoma to receive a new allegiance from these proud people, he did not understand the resentment they felt. The natives gave their oath and invited Oñate to visit one of their underground ceremonial chambers called "kivas." Something made Oñate hesitate and refuse to descend which may have saved his life. A few weeks later, one of Oñate's closest officers, Juan de Zaldivar with thirty men stopped by the pueblo and were invited in by the natives. Foolishly the Spaniards allowed themselves to be separated and all but four of them were brutally killed. Those who escaped did so by throwing themselves off the cliff. Juan de Zaldivar was not one of the survivors. When these four returned to report the massacre to Oñate, the governor weighed his options but realized that he could not let this revolt stand without punishment for fear it would encourage other pueblos to do the same. With the approval of the Counsel of the Friars,

Oñate sent Juan de Zaldivar's brother, Vicente with seventy men to punish the Acomese. The accounts of the battle on top of the mesa are disputed by several sources but what is clear is that the Spaniards, greatly outnumbered, waged a bloody battle and forced the natives to surrender.

There seems to be controversy as to the size of the population of Acoma at this time. In Oñate's report, he estimated the population to be about 3,000. Adolph Bandelier estimated the population to have been about 1,000. At any rate, it was a bloody slaughter. The captives, numbering perhaps 80 men and 500 women and children were returned to San Juan where a "trial" ensued. Oñate sentenced all the captives between the ages of 12 and 25 to twenty years of personal servitude and he condemned males older than 25 to have one foot severed. In Renaissance Europe, this was not an uncommon punishment. As a lesson to others who might be tempted to defy the Crown, Oñate carried out the mutilations in public.

Ten years after he departed for his governorship in New Mexico, Oñate was depleted of his money, reviled by his followers and accused of heinous crimes. He took it upon himself to resign. In his own defense, Oñate wrote:

"Unable to overcome my zeal and good purpose, the devil has exhausted my resources and I find myself unable to explore any further at a moment when the reports are most promising and encouraging."

The first governor of New Mexico and colonizer of the land north of Mexico goes down in history as something less than a conquistador. He is remembered by many for his brutality and greed.

6

Education in the Church

Well into the last century, formal education was reserved for the wealthy. This is still true in many parts of the world today. Of that small population, only the male members of the family were considered worthy of schooling. It may be argued that informal education takes place all the time, but the schooling of a gentleman was more formally provided. Most often it was the Church that taught the tenets of religion, language—including Latin and Greek and philosophy, when this did not contradict its own teachings.

By our standards today, we might consider the educated man of the early sixteen hundreds to be poorly prepared for roles of leadership. The question of educating the poor never arose and since there was no middle class, the wealthy cornered the market. In matters of teaching good hygiene, for example, the poor were again disadvantaged—although the upper class was not that far upstream.

The poor had the dictates of the church and the civil authority both of which demanded obedience. From the earliest age, the poor were taught to respect their betters and it was not difficult to know that a man on horseback was to be held in awe. The very name of gentleman in Spanish denotes a man on horseback—*caballero*. The slightest disrespect or perceived disrespect toward a caballero would earn the transgressor the flat side of a sword across his back. While might may often still be right in the modern world, it took at least two great revolutions to get the average man to accept the fact that the disadvantaged could and, indeed, should be taught. In later centuries, the redbrick universities in England and the state colleges in America grew as a response to this conviction.

At the time when Spain was expanding its reach across the seas, it was the attitude of the invaders that helped impose their will. They demanded only what they believed was their due. Much of what we consider today to be cruel and needlessly overbearing behavior was not considered so at the time. The native populations of New Mexico had no such frame of reference. They were not raised in a two-tier system of the haves and the have-nots.

"Why would these strangers take our food?" The natives might ask. "Let them grow their own." So it was not through reasoning that they would understand but rather through force. The native populations understood force, for hadn't they themselves imposed their might on weaker tribes and taken what they wanted from them? We can speculate as to what kind of world the Spanish would have created in New Mexico had they led by positive example rather than by brute force. On both sides we've seen glimmers of the goodness that was innate in their natures had they not allowed other imperatives to interfere. The natives were curious and generous with the first foreigners they saw, bringing them food and drink. The settlers taught the natives about other plants that would do well in the dry soil other than their native maize, squash and corn.

The Spaniards, however, did not seem committed for the long haul. The civil and religious leaders had pressing agendas of their own. The civil authorities were being judged by the amount of riches they could bring into the coffers of the Crown. The religious leaders were counting the souls they had saved from the fires of hell.

To speculate then is an exercise in futility. The parties played the roles they were given, dictated by the era in which they lived and the conditions by which they were defined.

7

Don Pedro de Peralta

At about the time when Jamestown, Virginia was being established, King Philip III of Spain was considering vacating the province of New Mexico. The year was 1608. The king was dissuaded by his viceroy in Mexico who reported that more than 7,000 natives had been converted to Christianity and their souls would indeed be in jeopardy without the continued blessings of holy sacraments.

In 1609, the king appointed Don Pedro de Peralta to be the new governor. Many consider Peralta to be the first governor of New Mexico, as they clearly write off Oñate as a spoiler and a cruel and corrupt businessman. The first capital, nevertheless, had been established on the Chama River where Oñate built San Gabriel. When Peralta was selected to become the governor of New Mexico, he was told to move the capital to a more central place, where he would not displace any native settlements. The Royal City of the Holy Faith or Santa Fe was established on the banks of a full-flowing river that was to take the name of the city.

The city was dedicated to its patron saint San Francisco d'Assisi. Under the combined rule of Ferdinand and Isabella in 1492, another Santa Fe had been built beside the city of Granada, Spain. Granada was the last Moorish stronghold remaining as the Christians drove the Moors from the peninsula. Unwilling to destroy the city because of its marvelous architecture, the Catholic Monarchs decided to use this Santa Fe de Granada to establish a siege to force out the Moors.

It worked. Now the city of Santa Fe, New Mexico would have a similar role—displace or convert the pagans.

Although no natives lived on the site selected by Peralta for the city, ancestors of the Pueblo Indians populated this site between 3,000 B.C and 600 A.D. Perhaps they left in search of more abundant water supplies. It is to Peralta that we owe our thanks for the Plaza, which extended originally up to the Cathedral and the Palace of Governors, constructed in 1610-12. The Palace is today the oldest government building in the United States.

The Plaza

The social life of the city would revolve around the plaza. The plaza was similar in design to about 11,000 other Spanish plazas throughout the Americas as ordered by a decree of the Law of the Indies. Its recommended dimensions were 600 feet by 400 feet and that eight streets were to run from it—two from each corner and one from the center of each long side. In addition to serving as a meeting place for the citizens of the city, the plaza was used by the army as a drill field for the soldiers. It may be difficult to imagine, seeing the plaza today, that at various times it was a dusty field, turning to mud in the winter, an extension of a local farm and covered with cornstalks or a grazing field for livestock.

As a point of comparison, Santa Fe was founded ten years before the Pilgrims landed on Plymouth Rock and is the oldest capital in the nation. Curiously having the oldest capital, New Mexico was one of the last states to be accepted into the Union. This was mostly due to the attitude of Congress that believed the Spanish language and culture of New Mexico were definitely non-American. There was also the matter of Congress being unwilling to upset the balance of slave versus free states that kept New Mexico out of consideration. It was only when the xenophobia subsided a bit that New Mexico was admitted to the Union as the 47th state in 1912.

At the high point of the city, beyond the river on the southeast side was the *Barrio de Analco*, which means "neighborhood on the other side". This is where the Mexican slaves who accompanied Peralta to Santa Fe were to be housed in their own neighborhood. For purposes of their own worship, a church was built in 1610. This church, named "San Miguel," was built on the ruins of an old native kiva. For that reason, San Miguel is said to have the oldest church foundations in the United States.

Sensitive to all the complaints that had been made about Oñate, the Viceroy Don Luis de Velasco gave specific orders to Peralta in dealing with the natives: "Inasmuch as it has been reported that the tribute levied on the natives is excessive, and that it is collected with much vexation and trouble to them, we charge the governor to take suitable measures in this matter, proceeding in such a way as to relieve and satisfy the royal conscience."

The viceroy went on to tell Peralta that the security of the settlers was foremost and that any trouble with the Indians should be handled peacefully if possible but by force if necessary.

During a time of relative peace with the Pueblo Indians, the community was caught in an internal conflict between the civil authority of the governor and the religious authority of the Church. It was also a time of great construction. Peralta occupied himself with the building of the Palace of the Governors while the Franciscan prelate of the New Mexico Missions, Alonso de Peinado, supervised the building of a church for Santa Fe. By 1640, the church had collapsed—it was constructed of mud mortar. It was not until two hundred years later that a strongly-build cathedral, Saint Francis, would appear on the same site.

The Palace of the Governors

The Palace of the Governors, more solidly built, was designed in the Spanish Colonial Style—one story with an overhanging portico to provide shade from the sun and protection from the rains. The flat roof was supported by exposed vigas. The walls were in most places three feet thick, which kept the Palace cool in the summer and warm in the winter. The windows in the first structure were narrow to protect the inhabitants from having more than one invader enter at a time, in the event of an assault. There was no glass for the windows but in time sheets of mica were used to allow the rays of sunlight to enter. Artifacts have been found from the 17th century about 18 inches below the present floor of the Palace. It is believed that this was due to soil erosion by rainwater over the centuries. Although viewing the Palace today, we have a good idea of the original structure; the Palace of 1612 was larger and was to change in design many times during the following centuries.

In 1772, for example, The Palace was modified as a new presidio with an open rectangle to accommodate a garrison of troops, which gave it the air of a military installation. In 1850 a territorial style porch was added. A hard stucco façade was added in 1872. U.S. Marshall John Sherman ordered a complete remodeling of the Palace's façade in 1877. A plank sidewalk was added; the porch posts were wrapped in elaborate moldings and each capped with a heavy cornice. In 1909, the New Mexico legislature made the Palace as an official headquarters building with an annual appropriation of $5,000. *The New Mexican* called the establishing of a museum in the Palace a magnificent idea. It would not be just of local interest but national and even international interest.

As a result of the arrival of the railway to New Mexico in 1878, tourism increased and with it a sense of nostalgia for the past. It was this sentiment that moved architect and photographer Jesse Nusbaum in 1912 to return the Palace to the style he believed it had originally been. Gone was the Greek Revival Style porch and with it went the Victorian colonnade. Today the Palace of the Governors as a museum is or should be on everyone's must-see list. Under the portal, on most days, one can see native Pueblo Indian vendors. In the late 1970s, a graduate student in law protested that it was racial discrimination to allow only Pueblo Indians to display their wares in front of the Palace.

He filed a lawsuit when he could not display his jewelry there. By making the Indians an integral part of the museum, the director managed to defeat the lawsuit. Each day the Indians take part in a lottery to determine who will have the opportunity to display their wares that day, since there are many more artisans than spaces in front of the museum.

Palace of the Governors, Santa Fe, NM, ca. 1885 (Courtesy Museum of New Mexico, Neg. #57077), Photo by Dana B. Chase

Discord between Church and State

Often bad chemistry between individuals is enough to spark serious discord. So it was when in late summer of 1612 a new prelate was appointed to replace Friar Peinado. From Mexico City came Friar Isidro Ordonez with ideas quite firm about his role in the society of Santa Fe. Joseph Sanchez writes: "Everyone knew Friar Ordonez's presence spelled trouble. When Governor Peralta heard Ordonez had replaced Peinado, he was heard to exclaim, 'Would to God the devil were coming instead of that friar!'"

The authenticity of the documents assigning Ordonez was in question and was considered by some of the friars to be forgeries. Ordonez was not a stranger to Santa Fe. He had served under Oñate and was hated by many. When Ordonez took it upon himself to order tribute collectors to return to Santa Fe from Taos, after Peralta had ordered them there, a serious break took place between them. Again Sanchez describes the situation: "The break between Friar Ordonez and Governor Peralta occurred in May 1613, when the prelate interfered with the governor's privileged functions to collect the annual tribute of corn and blankets from the pueblos. As the tribute collectors bound for Taos went past Nambe Pueblo, north of Santa Fe, Ordonez intercepted them, and under threat of excommunication, ordered them to return to the villa to hear mass, for the Feast of the Pentecost was at hand. Upon their return, Captain Pedro Ruiz, leader of the tribute collectors, reported to the governor, who ordered them back on the trail."

This was clearly a contest between two strong leaders. Ordonez would not accept the authority of the governor or at least considered that authority subordinate to his own. Ordonez threatened the governor with excommunication unless he ordered the tribute collectors to return. Peralta refused which initiated a series of acts—including putting a letter of excommunication on the door of the church, and throwing the governor's chair out of the church. Insults following insults, the drawing of arms and the accidental wounding of a priest brought the fever of discord to an uncontrollable level. Angered, Ordonez mounted the pulpit and spoke clearly to the congregation: "Do not be deceived. Let no one persuade himself with vain words that I do not have the same power and authority that the Pope in Rome has, or that if his Holiness were here in New Mexico, he could do more than I. Believe you that I can arrest, cast into irons, and punish as seems fitting to me any person without exception who is not obedient to the commandments of the church or mine."

It may be difficult to understand the great power of the Catholic Church from our present-day perspective. As a result of his insults against the church, Peralta was taken prisoner as he was making his way south. He was held in a cell for eight months before he escaped. The governor was weak and tired and attempted to hide but was found by Ordonez's men. He was imprisoned for another year when news came from Mexico City that a new governor had been named.

Even when the new governor, don Bernardino de Ceballos, entered New Mexico in the spring of 1614, he was forced to acknowledge the power of Ordonez. With the establishment of the Inquisition in New Mexico in 1626, a series of investigations took place, which revealed much abuse on the part of the civil government but also abuse among the clergy. The first agent of the Inquisition, Fray Alonso de Benevides, proved to be "a model of reason and moderation." Because of his correspondence and his book, *Memorial,* we have such a good knowledge of life in Santa Fe at that period. From his writings we read: "They (the congregation) lacked a church, as their first one had collapsed. I built a very fine church for them, at which they, their wives, and children personally aided me considerably by carrying the materials and helping to build the walls with their own hands."

8

The Pueblo Revolt

As we have seen by the discord and the constant struggle for power between the civil and religious leaders, the Spanish community was, in the long run, the loser. The Spanish Inquisition continued to thrive in Santa Fe. The Holy Office accused more than one governor of crimes. Although Peralta was returned to Mexico in shame, he was later exonerated and Ordonez was reprimanded for his handling of the matter. Don Fernando Lopez de Mendizabal, governor of New Mexico (1656-61), was arrested, imprisoned and died in custody but was later absolved of his "crimes" by the Inquisition. It did not take much of an accusation on the part of the Church to have even the highest civil authority brought down. Had not a precedent been set? Lopez de Mendizabal was accused of being a practicing Jew because he and his wife bathed on the Sabbath. The Church was eager to review all accusations, for its own edification, and often saw that neighbor would accuse neighbor of blasphemy just because of property disputes.

Eighty years after the Spaniards came north from Mexico to make a permanent settlement in Santa Fe; the Pueblo Indians revolted and drove them out. We have touched on some of the reasons for the anger and frustration of the Indians. They did not like being made slaves of the invaders. They did not like having to accept the religion of the Catholic Church. During the great building projects of the Peralta years, they were severely under compensated for their work. Having once believed that the gods of the Spaniards were more powerful than their own gods, they now had second thoughts. The land was, in recent years, under a severe drought and the Christian God did not bring relief. The Indians were constantly observing the disputes among their masters and realized that it was weakness they saw not strength. The Indians lost respect for both civil and religious masters. Despite the laws that prohibited it, often their masters abused the Indian workers. To instill Christianity, the Spaniards often resorted to floggings, torture and even hanging.

In 1680, the Indians rebelled. There had been other smaller attempts but this time it was well organized. An Indian medicine man named "Popé" had planned for five years to bring this about. The authorities had disciplined him by public flogging but his determination was firm. From Taos to Isleta, with the exception of Santa Fe, the Indians communicated by knotted cords to indicate a timeline for the attack and slowly moved in from all sides on the capital. The countryside was devastated, the churches were burned and holy shrines were defiled. Homes were looted and about four hundred settlers—men, women and children, including priests were killed. The revolt began on Saturday, August 10th, on the Feast of San Lorenzo. In the early days of the revolt, the governor was not aware that anything was amiss. By August 15th, the city of Santa Fe was under siege. Refugees from the outlying areas came for protection to the Palace of the Governors. On the events of the Pueblo Revolt, David Weber writes: "Then, in a few weeks in the late summer of 1680, Pueblos destroyed the Spanish colony of New Mexico, coordinating their efforts, as they had never done before. Pueblos launched a well-planned surprise attack. From the kiva at Taos, Pueblo messengers secretly carried calendars in the form of knotted cords to participating pueblos. Each knot marked a day until the Pueblos would take up arms."

Unquestionably, Popé was behind the spirit and drive of this revolt. His focus was constant and his energy boundless. Those who fault him for his methods should remember our own American Revolution. We demanded freedom from the oppressor, as did the

Pueblo Indians. At least 20,000 Indians pledged themselves to the revolt. The uprising was scheduled for the night of the new moon but word leaked out. Two Christian Indians at Tesuque warned the governor and the date of the revolt was moved up.

Governor Otermin was caught off guard, as were many of the three thousand Spaniards spread along the Rio Grande. The Indians killed twenty-one of the thirty-three Franciscans. James relates these events when he wrote: "Instigated by their medicine-men, the Indians were particularly vindictive in their treatment of the padres. Father Juan Jesus, the oldest priest at Jemez, was awakened in the dead of night, was dragged from his bed and made to carry the Indians on his back, as he crawled on his hands and knees, until he fell dead. His body was cast out and devoured by wolves. At Acoma, the padre was stripped naked, dragged about the streets with a rope around his neck, then beaten to death with clubs."

Surrounding the Palace of the Governors and cutting off the water supply, the Indians gave the governor a choice—leave peacefully and return to Mexico under a white flag of truce or be put to death. The Spaniards fought hard, managing to drive off the Pecos and the Tanos but the Indians of the north continued the siege. Governor Otermin received two wounds, one in his face and the other in his chest. Another week passed and after trying once more to save his Palace, Governor Otermin finally surrendered. He walked out of the Palace with just under two thousand settlers and they made their way down to El Paso.

In 1681, Otermin received orders from the viceroy. He was to return to New Mexico to attempt to repossess it. He headed northward with a party of 147 soldiers. In a pitiful show of force, he burned what was unimportant and made a show of power without really having any. When the Pueblo Indians who had no intention of giving back what they had gained the year before faced Otermin with their own show of strength, Otermin gave up.

The Pueblo Revolt had been a success; the Pueblo People had won their independence—at least for the next twelve years. Between

1610 and 1680, there had been twenty-three governors to rule New Mexico. One governor—Juan Duran de Miranda served twice, but not consecutively. At the time of the revolt in 1680, three generations of Santa Feans had been born in the city and reached adulthood there. About 87% of the population were at this time natives of the province.

As a reaction to the religion that had been imposed on them, the Indians tried to bathe and rub off the holy water with which they had been baptized. Popé declared that all marriages made under Spanish rule would be considered wrong and had to be made again according to native tradition. Popé ordered that all plant life not native to the Pueblo Indians be torn up and burned. Those horses not taken by the fleeing Spaniards were turned out and allowed to run free, much to the delight of the Apache and Comanche Indians, who were in sore need of transportation for their raiding parties.

When Otermin later interrogated a Tano Indian known as Pedro Garcia, the governor wanted to know why the Indians had rebelled. Pedro said that the Pueblos were tired of all the work they had to do for the Spaniards and the missionaries. It rankled them that they did not have time to plant for themselves or to do other things they needed to do. When Governor Otermin interrogated another Indian, a Tiwa man from Alameda, the governor learned the resentment that the Indians felt was great . . . because the Spaniards took away their idols and forbade their sorceries and mocked their ancient customs. The governor later learned from Pueblo captives about Popé's administration of New Mexico: "He (Popé) ordered in all the pueblos through which he passed that they instantly break up and burn the images of the holy Christ, the Virgin Mary and other saints, the crosses and everything pertaining to Christianity."

There is not much reliable documentation of the years of the Pueblo rule in New Mexico. We do know that there were quarrels among the Indians when they no longer had the Spanish to subjugate them. With the Spanish gone, there was no more need among the Pueblos for unity. Popé was criticized for exhibiting some of the same traits that the Spanish governor had shown—overbearing and immovable in matters of his decisions.

The history of the Southwest has not been of great interest to American historians but those who are interested in the Southwest have regarded the Pueblo Revolt as a significant event. It was the only time in North America that an Indian revolt had been successful.

9

Don Diego de Vargas

The Reconquest and Failure

Spain had lost considerable money and prestige in its occupation of New Mexico. The King of Spain, Philip III had grown tired of the drain this venture had on his treasury. He would have much preferred to spend the money on court entertainment. Unlike his formidable father, Philip II who was always in control of events, Philip III allowed his ministers to make important decisions for him especially his favorite—Francisco Gomez de Sandoval.

It was a peculiar request to Sandoval then that a gentleman from an important Spanish family made to undertake the reconquest of New Mexico in a peaceful campaign. This was Don Diego de Vargas whose family had distinguished itself over the years as knights and crusaders, diplomats and bishops. Why would this handsome, wealthy man want to take on the hardships of life in New Mexico when he had all the advantages of a privileged existence in New Spain?

The viceroy in Mexico, Conde de Galve, tried to dissuade de Vargas from pursuing such a mission. Finally with permission of the viceroy, de Vargas made his way up the Camino Real as his predecessors had done before him over the dusty trails and up along the Rio Grande. Six months later, he arrived at his destination. It was September 1692.

Don Diego de Vargas, Painting (Courtesy Museum of New Mexico, Neg. #11409)

De Vargas led his men—soldiers and robed Franciscan friars—across the fields and plaza of the former Spanish capital. He gave orders to his men not to fire their weapons unless he unsheathed his sword. The Palace of the Governors had changed since being occupied by the Pueblo Indians—mostly from the Galisteo area.

The Indians had built a defensive wall around the Palace, which remained in place until de Vargas' successor Governor Cubero ordered it taken down.

The Indians had built several stories atop the Palace in their own style. Many Indians now lived within the Palace and they watched the procession with curiosity and some concern. With his helmet in his hand, astride his horse, de Vargas told the Indians through an interpreter that he had come in peace; that the King of Spain forgave them for the desecration of the holy shrines, the destruction of the churches and the killing of the priests and other Spaniards. He had come to have them renew their vows of obedience to the king—Almighty God's servant on earth.

Whether the Indians understood that this was a reconquest of New Mexico or not isn't clear but the bows that had been trained on de Vargas were lowered. De Vargas heard or thought he heard an agreement on the part of the Indians to accept his proclamation. With this he departed with all his men to seek a similar agreement from other tribes around the area and to gather the settlers down in El Paso who were bound for Santa Fe. Seventy families, many headed by widows, were prepared to return to Santa Fe, a total of about eight hundred people. In October 1693, after eight months of delay, they departed from El Paso.

When de Vargas returned to Santa Fe, it was the dead of winter and he set up tents around the plaza and approached the Indians again, reminding them of their agreement to accept the conditions he had outlined. The Indians refused to leave the Palace of the Governors. After two weeks of negotiations to no avail and facing his own problems with small children dying of exposure in the tents, de Vargas, though initially full of good intentions, finally resorted to a tried and true method of imposing his will. On the morning of December 29, 1693 a fierce battle broke out. The Pueblo Indians were not unified as they had been in 1680, to their disadvantage. The battle waged on all that day and in the morning, the Spaniards scaled the walls. Seeing no hope of victory, the Indian governor named "Jose" hanged himself. By afternoon, the battle was over. What de Vargas had not been able to take by negotiation, he took by force and punished the Indians who had opposed him—about seventy men. The rest of the region was secured in rapid order.

Before he had taken the city by force, back in the fall when he was still content with his peaceful reconquest, de Vargas had written a dispatch to Mexico City announcing his bloodless triumph. It is this that history selectively remembers and even today a holiday is celebrated in honor of the Virgin of the Rosary or commonly known as "La Conquistadora" (Our Lady of Triumph) who helped de Vargas in his "bloodless" victory. The banner of the King of Spain floated once again above the Palace of the Governors.

Unfortunately, the man who had wanted so badly to go to New Mexico wanted as desperately to move on to more prestigious assignments and petitioned as much from the king. He suggested that Manila in the Philippines might be to his liking or even Guatemala. While his request was making its way through the bureaucracy of Mexico City and Spain, he changed his mind and decided to stay in New Mexico. Unhappily for him, it was his first request that was acted on and a new governor was designated for New Mexico.

Pedro Rodriguez Cubero had long coveted the post of governor. He, at last, had his wishes fulfilled. With the aim to discredit the former governor, Cubero spread enough ill will and calumny around to get de Vargas imprisoned in one of the towers of the Palace. Many charges were leveled against de Vargas: misuse of royal funds, abuse of authority, favoritism and creating sedition among colonists and Indians.

Diego de Vargas was kept in a small cell in solitary confinement. No one in Mexico City or Spain knew of this imprisonment and Cubero prohibited all communication with and about de Vargas. While de Vargas was in captivity in Santa Fe, he was being honored in Spain. In 1698, the king granted him a noble title. At last in 1700, de Vargas was released from prison. He then traveled to Mexico City to live quietly with friends. Two years later, he was finally exonerated of all accusations against him. In 1704, after his death, an inventory was made of his possessions. It was revealed that he owned forty-one books—an astonishingly large number by the standards of the day. Another governor in the nineteenth century—Lew Wallace—would also prove to be a man of letters. Curiously, both would be eager to leave Santa Fe.

With the reconquest, more Spaniards came to New Mexico seeking land. A land-grant system was devised to accommodate the new arrivals. The Pueblo Indians and the Spaniards lived in relative peace in the following years. Attacks, however, from the Apaches and the Navajos and increasingly from the Comanches continued. In the ensuing years, Spain became less concerned with New Mexico as its attention was drawn to the growing threats of the French and Indians in Texas. Just as Spain expanded into Texas in response to a foreign threat, so it acquired western Louisiana for purely defensive reasons. With rumors that the French were operating among the Pawnee Indians in the central plains, a young lieutenant from Santa Fe named Don Pedro de Villasur took a small army and started to explore the area northeast of the Platte River in present-day Nebraska. The Pawnees fell upon the expedition and killed more than thirty soldiers, among them was Villasur. Governor Valverde was criticized for having sent such an inexperienced young lieutenant on such a hazardous mission. A fine was imposed on the governor of fifty pesos to pay for charity masses for the souls of the dead soldiers.

More importantly, this event made the French see the vulnerability of the Spanish on one hand and the possibility of extending their trade, which they hoped, would bring, in payment for their goods, silver from the mines of Chihuahua. The Spanish, on their side, became more resolved to strengthen their defenses and not allow any contact at all with the French. The borders would remain sealed to foreigners.

The 18th century was a time for growth and development for New Mexico. There was considerable trading on the Camino Real. The settlers awaited the arrival of the supply caravan from Mexico with great anticipation. It arrived, as records show, approximately every three years.

The population in Santa Fe doubled to 2,542 residents during the century. It was noted that among the changes that had taken place among the settlers, there was the change in language. The linguistic phenomenon was that with little contact with the outside Spanish-speaking world, the Spanish language had become more countrified. Vocabulary became simplified; Indian words were adopted. The overall effect was that the manner of speaking became less graceful and less courtly.

In the late 1700s and early 1800s, Spain was distracted by its other possessions in the Southwest. The great impact of the Spanish presence in the Southwest, from Texas to California has been well documented in matters of language, religion and culture. But the land and its natives also had a powerful impact on the Spaniards. For example, the Spaniards came from a land that was very arid in parts but never did they find the need to deal with desert conditions like those in New Mexico. From the natives, they learned the judicious use of that precious commodity—water. In the high mountain villages of New Mexico, the paucity of farmland and the need to share water put a premium on cooperation and intensified communitarian traditions, including communal ownership of land. In the wide Rio Grande Valley, south of Santa Fe, richness of soil and abundance of water fostered large privately-owned lands. Across most of the Spanish rim, the demands of frontier life forced a high percentage of Hispanics, even those with unpaid servants, to work their own land and tend to their own livestock, learning techniques and shortcuts from the natives.

Even protecting themselves from the raiding Apaches, the Spaniards had a common bond with the Pueblo Indians. Unlike the English settlers of the Northeast who had little sustained contact with the local Indian tribes, Spaniards remained in close contact with the Pueblo Indians. Spanish women learned to plaster their adobe houses from the Indians. The Spaniards learned how to use locally procured drugs which were previously unknown to them.

The greatness of the Spanish Empire under Philip II became less extended under his son Philip III. Sustaining such an enormous presence in the Americas cost money. The Church was eager to spend the king's riches as long as the clergy were building churches and saving souls. The empire had grown too big and unmanageable. Spain had trouble at home and wars were costly.

In 1786, Bernardo de Galvez devised a new policy for dealing with the warring Indians in New Mexico. He had learned this from the French and English on the Apache frontier in Louisiana several years before. His policy was to use trade rather than war to maintain harmonious relations with the natives. It was important to make the

Indians dependent on the Spaniards for satisfying their needs. This included selling the Indians guns and gunpowder and making them dependent for procuring these new arms.

Under Juan Bautista Anza, Governor of New Mexico from 1778 to 1787, a policy of conciliation and negotiation replaced force as the cornerstone of this new association with the Indians.

It was Governor Anza who had forged a lasting peace with the western Comanches who had been such a threat to the province for so many years. Anza could not blame the settlers from spreading themselves out along the fertile banks of the Rio Grande but he felt that he could not give adequate protection to these people. Every time the Indians raided the farms, the settlers would demand protection from the army. Anza had long believed that urban renewal was needed to provide the citizens of New Mexico with security. He developed a plan for moving all the settlers up from their homes along the Rio Grande and housing them on the high ground south of the Santa Fe River. When the citizens heard of this plan, they complained loudly to Mexico City and the development never took place.

Although the Inquisition had put into effect a ban on any foreigner entering the province without permission, Governor Fernando de la Concha defied the ban by having dealings with Frenchmen from New Orleans. He was accused of being a heretic and in front of witnesses he once said, "The masses said by New Mexico friars were worth about as much as what my horse might say."

Mining

Although Coronado did not find streets glistening with gold as he had hoped and Oñate could not coax silver from the earth, mines did exist in New Mexico as early as 1685. The first mining activity of lasting importance began in 1804 in the copper deposits of Santa Rita, in the southwestern part of the state. In 1828, gold was discovered in the Ortiz Mountains between Albuquerque and Santa Fe. This remains today the oldest gold-mining area in the United States.

On October 19,1903, the newspaper headlines read: "Bonanza near Capital City. Gold and Silver Vein Seven Feet Wide and Six Thousand Feet Long Struck Four Miles Northeast of the Plaza. Gold Runs Ninety-Nine Percent to One of Silver."

By the time New Mexico became a territory of the United States, annual gold production was valued at three million dollars.

From the beginning of mining in the state, Indians worked the mines and foreigners were prohibited from mining activity. There is a story of an Indian who fell sick and was taken to Fort Union for medical care. He later returned with a pretty rock to give as payment for his care. The rock contained gold and a rush soon began to the area. Discovery after discovery took place and soon twenty-three of the state's thirty-two counties were mining gold. The areas northeast of Taos, northeast of Santa Fe and in the southwestern corner of the state are the most important concentrations. The Spanish conquistadors were not wrong about gold; unfortunately, they arrived too early on the scene.

Silver, so eagerly sought by Oñate throughout the New Mexico Province and as far west as California, was not found until 1863 in Magdalena and Socorro. Silver City was to become the center of the silver mining activity. Grant County became the center of copper mining and much later, lead and zinc made their appearance in the state.

There is no way of knowing how long the residents of New Mexico used coal for heating. We know that during the Civil War coal was used in the army camps for fuel. In Colfax County near Raton, the first real activity of coal mining took place. The arrival of the railroads between 1879 and 1882 put coal mining on a solid footing.

Zebulon Pike

With the Louisiana Purchase in 1803, Thomas Jefferson had stretched the United States Constitution around the sprawling Louisiana territory, which was still poorly defined. This was the disputed territory that the French had ceded to Spain in 1762 rather than let it fall into the hands of the British. A year later, Lewis and Clark were outfitting and making their preparations.

In 1806, a good deal of attention was being given to the holdings of Spain in the Southwest. One aspect of the infamous Burr conspiracy was to bring riches to the plotters by despoiling the Spanish empire in America. Enter Zeb Pike, a young U.S. Army lieutenant who enjoyed exploration but was not particularly politically astute. He has been called a "poor man's Lewis and Clark."

Pike, son of a veteran of the American Revolution, had orders to investigate the sources of the Arkansas and Red Rivers. With twenty-three men, he crossed the plains to the foot of the Rockies. Most Americans know only that a mountain peak in Colorado is named after him. Whether he was a knowing foil in the hands of his superior, General Wilkinson, or not isn't fully known. The General sent Zebulon Pike on an extended information-gathering mission into the Spanish-controlled Southwest. Pike and his companion, Dr. John Hamilton Robinson had concocted a false reason of wanting to collect a debt in Santa Fe.

Little is known about the real mission of Robinson who ostensibly tipped off the Spaniards they were coming. The fiction of debt collection was created in order to protect Robinson from being held as a spy in the event of war between Spain and the United States. Once the party passed the Sangre de Cristo Mountains, there was no doubt that they were in Spanish territory. It is hard to believe that Pike mistook the Rio Grande for the Red River as he later claimed. Pike was to construct a fort and fly an American flag in the Spanish territory—another ploy to claim that land in the event of war. Spain jealously guarded its borders to Texas and New Mexico from outsiders. The Commander of the Internal Provinces of New Spain, Nemesio Salcedo had Pike and party arrested and interred in the Palace of the Governors, despite Pike's claim that they had lost their way.

On March 3, 1807, the following exchange took place between Pike and the governor of New Mexico:

Governor: Do you speak French?

Pike: Yes, sir.

Governor: You come to reconnoiter our country, do you?

Pike: I marched to reconnoiter our own.

Governor: In what character are you?

Pike: In my proper character, an officer of the United States Army.

One credible scenario is that Wilkinson's desire was to have them apprehended so that they could bring back valuable information about the Spanish fortifications. He was undoubtedly convinced that Spain would release the party unharmed rather than risk military confrontation with the United States. The party was then marched southward into the interior but Pike and his men were later returned to the borders of Louisiana by way of Texas.

Between 1807 and 1821, due to the exploration of Zebulon Pike, several Americans attempted trade in New Mexico and to trap in the streams. The mountain men or trappers were the precursors of the heavy influx of American immigrants. These men were of many different races and cultural backgrounds. They knew no borders or boundaries but moved freely as they pleased. It was not just to New Mexico that they traveled but also throughout the Southwest. They led a rough and dangerous life and oral history abounds with their pursuits. They trapped beaver for the pelts and all but depleted the supply. Trapping and trading, they gradually and steadily pushed the limits of civilization westward well into Spanish territory.

In the first two decades of the nineteenth century, Spain's New World Empire crumbled. In 1821, New Spain (Mexico) declared its independence from Spain, following the other former Spanish colonies. This placed most of what is now the American West, including all of Nevada, Utah and parts of Colorado, Kansas and Wyoming, as well as the four border states of California, Arizona, New Mexico and Texas, under the jurisdiction of independent Mexico. Thomas James described the celebration of Mexico's independence from Spain. He tells how it was his idea to erect a seventy-foot liberty pole and run up the first flag: "No Italian carnival ever exceeded this celebration in thoughtlessness, vice and licentiousness of every description."

Governor Melgares called it an unforgettable day. There were salvos, processions and pageants and Indian dances in the plaza.

In late 1827, there were rumors that Spain planned to invade and reconquer Mexico. In preparation of this eventuality, the Mexican National Congress decreed the expulsion of peninsular Spaniards from the republic. Several Spanish Franciscans left New Mexico as a result.

This was to be a short-term reality. Texas, seeing the opportunity to avenge the loss of lives at the Alamo and seek independence for Texas rebelled successfully against Mexico in 1836. Ten years later, in 1846, American troops invaded New Mexico, southern Arizona and California.

As a backdrop, the stage had been set for the Mexican Independence. The French Revolution and Napoleonic Wars diverted Spain's attention from its colonies. Ferdinand VII was removed from the Spanish throne and was replaced by Joseph Bonaparte, Napoleon's brother. One name stands out among many important figures of this period. He was called the leader of the movement for Mexican Independence—Father Miguel Hidalgo y Costilla, a liberal priest form the Parish of Delores. It was Father Hidalgo who distributed the *Grito de Delores*—a call for social and economic reform. In an attempt to gain more supporters for his cause he said: "My friends and countrymen: Neither the king nor tributes exist for us any longer. We have borne this shameful tax, which only suits slaves, for three centuries as a sign of tyranny and servitude; a terrible stain, which we shall know how to wash away . . ."

Before he was executed in 1811, Father Hidalgo was made to recant by the Inquisitors. In a statement he said: "I am repentant for the incalculable ills which have originated out of the frenzy which possessed me to break so scandalously with the King, the nation and Christian morality."

10

The Santa Fe Trail

During the years of Spanish control of New Mexico, the Spanish regime was very restrictive about trade. New Mexico could only trade with Mexico, which was designed to keep the proceeds within the provinces. All overtures from the United States or France were discouraged. The towns south of Santa Fe on the Camino Real such as El Paso and Chihuahua began to thrive with trade. Arriving about this same time in the Santa Fe area were the mountain men.

When Mexico declared its independence from Spain in 1821, it took possession of New Mexico as well. That same year trade was encouraged and began to grow with the United States.

Governor Facundo Melgares foresaw the great possibilities of opening the pathway to the northeast, although the prairie was not without danger and risk.

In 1821, William Becknell, of Franklin, Missouri advertised for men to accompany him to the southern Rockies for the purpose of trading horses and mules and catching wild animals. Unknown to Becknell was the fact that the lands he wished to visit were no longer in the hands of the Spanish and the very restrictive trade laws they enforced. At a place near Raton Pass, Becknell and his men were stopped by Mexican soldiers who escorted the startled men from Missouri into Santa Fe.

The city was in full celebration of the independence of Mexico from Spain. Instead of selling horses, he sold everything else he had in his wagons including calico and various sundry items that had been unavailable prior to this time in Santa Fe. Seeing an excellent possibility for business, Becknell returned again to Santa Fe, this time with three freight wagons and a pack train loaded with $5,000 worth of merchandise and again turned a handsome profit. William Becknell is known today as the "Father of the Santa Fe Trail" for his pioneering spirit and sound business sense.

With his success, many wagons began to travel the long journey from Missouri to Santa Fe. The concerns were many. The shorter of the two trails was the southern route, which led through the Cimarron Desert. The advantages were that the wagons could negotiate the desert paths more easily but there was a lack of water and the danger of Indian raids was greater. The northern route through the Colorado passes was free from Indian concerns and there was plenty of water but the mountain passes were so difficult that at times, the wagons had to be lowered over the cliffs by rope.

Augustus Storrs who later became the first US Consul for Santa Fe turned an investment of $35,000 into $180,000 by trading.

An important person of trade and commerce of this period was Josiah Gregg. His writings have contributed greatly to the understanding and appreciation of the Southwest. His book *Commerce of the Prairies* is a classic. It was Gregg who brought the first printing press to the territory.

Trade on the Santa Fe Trail became so important to the economy of the region that an attempt was made to pay the Indians for the right of passage through their lands. The Kiowas and Comanches had been raiding and killing so many of the traders. The Indians took the money but paid no attention to the treaty. It was not until 1828 that military escorts began to accompany the wagons to assure their safe arrival. The traders on the trail would elect a captain of the caravan whose powers were undefined and vague but had the responsibility of directing the travel, selecting the camping sites and making general decisions on a daily basis. All members of the caravan were required to stand guard duty. When the party had crossed the dangerous plains, the organization was dissolved.

As a byproduct of the heavy trade with Santa Fe, other markets, further south also benefited from the goods coming from the north, as long as peace existed between the Anglos of Missouri and the Mexicans. Santa Fe became the nucleus of trade, rather than the end of the line. At the height of the trade on the Santa Fe Trail in 1846, just before General Kearny acquired the region in a bloodless takeover, a total of 628 wagons carried just under a million dollars of goods. The wagons would often assume a military formation, sometimes ten or more wagons abreast as they crossed the wide plains. There was security in numbers.

As a child of seven, Marion Sloan Russell arrived in Santa Fe in 1852. She later described her first impressions: "How our hearts waited for a sight of Santa Fe of our dreams. We thought it would be a city and waited breathlessly for the first sight of towers and tall turrets. We crossed a water ditch . . . then passed a great wooden gateway that arched high above us. We were in Santa Fe."

Danger was ever-present on the trail. In her diary, Susan Shelby Magoffin told how her brother James had been robbed of everything he owned by the Apache Indians but was lucky to have his life spared. This was unusual because the scalp was considered the finest trophy. There is also the story about James White who was a merchant of Independence, Missouri and Santa Fe. In October 1849, while traveling with his wife and young daughter, he was attacked by Apache Indians—at a place where the caravan was supposed to be out of danger. All eight men in the caravan were killed and the woman and child were taken captive. When the murder was reported, Kit Carson and some other guides tried to rescue the woman and her child but as they were speaking with the Indians, the woman began to run toward her rescuers but was immediately killed by the Apaches. The child was never found.

Clearly other travelers from the East were surprised to find such primitive living conditions in their adopted city of Santa Fe. Settlers from Europe, especially from Germany were among the founding fathers of the city's mercantile businesses. Excellent books have been written about the German-Jewish pioneers and how they worked hard and gave generously to the growth of the city, whether it was in support of Archbishop Lamy's construction of St. Francis Cathedral or the pledge to bring the railroad to Santa Fe.

The first of these merchants was Jacob Solomon Spiegelberg who arrived with General Kearny in New Mexico in 1846. Solomon Bibo had come to Santa Fe from Germany at the age of sixteen. So completely did he integrate himself into his new life that he married the granddaughter of a prominent Acoma governor, spoke Keresan, Navajo, and Zuni along with his Native German. Acoma was the first and only pueblo to elect a non-Indian governor—Solomon Bibo. In passing, some of the names that were prominent in this regard over the years are: Nathan Bibo and family; Willi and Flora Spiegelberg, Felix and Susan Warburg, Jacob Amberg, Gustave Elsberg, the Zeckendorf brothers, the Staabs and many, many others.

The Santa Fe Trail was the only easy route between the Rowe bluffs and the Sangre de Cristo Mountains for those making their way to Pueblo Indian country. This passage had been used for thousands of years as a main trade route between the Great Plains and the Rio Grande. Later the Atchison, Topeka and Santa Fe Railway followed this route.

11

Unrest, Rebellion and War

In 1835, Colonel Albino Perez was sent by officials in Mexico to take charge of the departmental affairs of New Mexico. Governor Perez was a man of high ideals and excellent plans for public education. Santa Feans disliked him. He was not a native and the changes he brought were unpopular. To make matters worse, the governor had to impose new tax laws.

This brought about a revolt. It began in the Chimayo-Santa Cruz de la Canada area north of Santa Fe. Perez was unable to put down the uprising. He fled the capital, was caught and assassinated near Agua Fria. What had started out as a plan to support public education in New Mexico by direct taxation progressed to mandates for punishment of nonperformance of military education and then ended with the killing of the messenger. It was a brutal death at that—decapitation with Perez's head carried around on a pike.

Manuel Armijo who had been governor of New Mexico was called upon to bring peace and order to New Mexico after the revolt. He was to punish the leaders and assume the functions of governor once again. The rebels had installed Jose Gonzalez to take the place of Perez. When Armijo took charge, Gonzalez was put to death, as were other leaders.

In 1841, a Texan incursion tested Armijo's resolve. The governor, however, was able to push back the Texans with little difficulty. The writing was now on the wall. The Americans were coming. Fully armed with a belief that Manifest Destiny was to be fulfilled—stretching

American soil from sea to sea—the United States was in a frenzy of land grabbing. Mexico, claiming that the United States had been a bad and greedy neighbor broke off diplomatic relations with the United States in March 1845.

Stephen Watts Kearny

Stephen Watts Kearny was born August 30, 1794 in Newark, New Jersey but lived in the West most of his years of service. He was a soldier, explorer, builder, writer and statesman. He commanded the Army of the West and was called the "Father of the US Cavalry."

In May 1846, Congress, at the urging of President Polk, declared war on Mexico. A month later, the Army of the West set out for New Mexico over the Santa Fe Trail. Leading the army was Brigadier-General Stephen Watts Kearny from Leavenworth Missouri. After

ten years in the West, Kearny had already become legendary, and his skill and fame as a leader was so extensive that men fought to fill the ranks of his army. Kearny had about 300 army regulars, most of them experienced in western duty and some inexperienced frontiersmen.

General Stephen Watts Kearny, Painting (Courtesy Museum of New Mexico, Neg. #9938)

Kearny had heard that a Mexican army of about 3,000 was marching north from Chihuahua. Kearny had no way of verifying this news but he did not want to waste any time. Leaving Fort Leavenworth, he kept his troops moving until they reached Bent's Fort. He had covered more than 550 miles.

On August 1st, Kearny wrote to Governor Armijo from Bent's Fort on the Arkansas River in present-day Colorado. He wrote: "By annexation of Texas to the United States, the Rio Grande from its mouth to its source forms. . . the boundary between her and Mexico, and I come by orders . . . to take possession of the country, over part of which you are now presiding as Governor . . ."

The letter held the proverbial carrot in one hand saying that all consideration would be made in the transfer of control in a "benevolent" manner and a whip in the other hand threatening reprisals and punishment should the United States forces encounter opposition. General Kearny sent two men to convince the governor to accept his terms without delay—Captain George Cooke and James W. Magoffin, a Santa Fe trader. In a letter to the Secretary of War, Magoffin wrote: "I found many of the rich of the Department here, also the militia officers, with whom I had ample intercourse. I assured them the only object of our Govmt. was take possession of New Mexico as being part of the territory annexed to the U.S. and to give peace and quietude to the good people of the country which gave them entire satisfaction."

Whatever words were exchanged during the meeting is not known. The fictionalized account of the card game between Armijo and Kearny, playing for the future of Santa Fe as related in this author's book *Pulling No Ponchos* was not meant to be taken seriously. Rumors still persist, although no proof exists, that Armijo was given a case of gold in exchange for not opposing the will of General Kearny. The following day, Armijo departed down the Camino Real with a bodyguard of soldiers instead of fighting for Santa Fe at Apache Pass. Unlike the Tewa Indians who were invited to lay down their arms by de Vargas, Armijo was a pragmatic businessman and knew how to evaluate a situation.

General Kearny entered Santa Fe without firing a single shot. With Armijo gone, acting governor, Juan Bautista Vigil y Alarid surrendered at the Palace of the Governors and the U.S. flag was raised over the Palace. General Kearny immediately went about scouting for a site upon which to build a fort. Marc Simmons writes: "Soldiers and hired workmen threw up thick adobe walls, 9 feet high and surrounded by a deep ditch. A log structure inside the compound provided a magazine for storing gunpowder."

General Kearny died on October 31, 1848 at the home of Major Merriwether Lewis Clark in St. Louis, Missouri. Kearny's military expeditions served to enlarge the territorial holdings of the United States by more than a million square miles.

Mexican Governor and General Manuel Armijo, Drawing by Clarence Batchelor (Courtesy Museum of New Mexico, Neg. #8790)

Fort Marcy, named for Secretary of War, William L. Marcy, was hurriedly built on the high ground north of the Plaza. It was never garrisoned and never used to defend Santa Fe.

It seems that the troops stationed at Fort Marcy were a constant concern to the citizens of the capital. Most of these troops were transferred to Fort Union in 1851. When Lt. Colonel Sumner took up his new assignment as commander of the Military Department of New Mexico, he showed his dismay in writing: "I reached Santa Fe, on the 19th of July and assumed post at Santa Fe, that sink of vice and extravagance, and to remove the troops and public property to this place (Fort Union)."

Fort Marcy was closed in 1867. With whatever ease General Kearny had in taking Santa Fe, all was not well. A number of the descendents of the Spanish settlers were upset about giving up Santa Fe to the Anglo-Americans. They felt more closely allied to Mexico. In December 1846, these prominent citizens plotted against the newly arrived Americans to undermine their authority. There are several stories about how the plot was discovered, suffice it to say that the Americans learned about it and arrested the plotters.

More serious was the Pueblo Indian reaction to the new governor of the New Mexico Territory. Incited to riot, these Indians attacked Governor Charles Bent in his Taos home, shot him with arrows and scalped him. Rosemary Nusbaum describes the holidays that the Bent brothers planned to have at Taos where Charles Bent who had recently been appointed governor of the territory by General Kearny was to meet with his family: "William Bent decided to go to Taos for a few days of rest with his Mexican wife Ignacia and their three children. At the time, Kit Carson's wife Josefa was staying with them. Bent (the new governor) knew there were no troops in Taos. At dawn on January 19th, a howling mob of Mexican and Indian supporters came to the house. He (Bent) stepped outside and an arrow killed him."

It is uncertain whether this act was directed against the Bents—Charles, William and George or whether it was the way the Taos Indians wanted to show their special welcome for the new American regime. The revolt spread quickly but the army responded without hesitation. In late January 1847, following the battles at Santa Cruz de la Canada and Embudo, the rebels retreated. On February 3rd, the insurrection was broken and many prisoners were taken. The prisoners were tried for treason and murder and many were hanged.

With the arrival of the American Army and the building of Fort Marcy, many more settlers flowed into Santa Fe. Bars and gambling houses became the gathering places for these new arrivals. The strictly religious nature of the capital as it had flourished under Spanish and Mexican rule was changing. The cultural clash of Anglo-American and Hispanic American became evident. It was in 1850 that Congress recognized the territorial status of New Mexico, although General Kearny had declared it unofficially earlier. It was also the first year that New Mexico petitioned for statehood but was ignored.

In putting the war between the United States and Mexico into the perspective of more than a hundred and fifty years, we see that Americans still call it the "Mexican War" while Mexicans refer to it as the "U.S. Invasion." Even the most casual reader of history cannot help but conclude that the United States was bent on fighting Mexico for land.

On April 25, 1846, the opportunity presented itself. Mexico had given the US the excuse it needed. Mexican soldiers under the command of General Mariano Arista crossed the Rio Grande and attacked an American patrol, killing or wounding sixteen men. This was the opportunity President Polk was waiting for. In his war message to Congress on May 11th, he said: "Mexico . . . has invaded our territory and shed American blood upon American soil."

Very quickly American armies invaded Mexico, crossing its northern frontier and eventually moving inland from its eastern coast. When General Winfield Scott marched his army from Veracruz to Mexico City, the war was over. In a treaty, the US paid Mexico $15,000,000 and for that sum received the vast northern provinces of California and New Mexico and recognized the Rio Grande as the international border.

Under the new American regime, the nomad tribes were being defeated and confined to reservations. The Pueblo people were finding it difficult to adjust to American rule. Whatever privilege they may have enjoyed under the Mexican regime was not at all guaranteed under the Americans. Of major concern was the protection of rights and property of the Pueblo Indians. There was so little understanding of the Native Americans in Washington and little willingness to see the difference between the peaceful Pueblo people and the war-like nomads. These concerns were some of the first to be addressed by New Mexico's first Indian agent, James S. Calhoun.

With the Treaty of Guadalupe Hidalgo, protection was also assured to those persons who became citizens of the United States. However, respecting the land grant arrangements made by the Spaniards or Mexicans proved to be more complicated than the Americans originally thought. First of all, there was a clear difference between the systems of law pertaining to property. Although the U.S. Government had pledged by treaty to honor pre-existing Spanish and Mexican land grants, the reality was much more difficult. The custom of handing the new owner a handful of dirt in front of witnesses was a common practice in Europe and often there were no written documents of the sale. Where written documents existed, the language was often difficult to understand because of the age of the document or the illiteracy of the person writing it. The concept of ownership was also different. Boundary lines were indistinct, often described in ambiguous terms. Properties had never been surveyed or even measured. Often, original documents had been lost or consumed in a fire. Hand copies were often not reliable. The lack of clarity concerning claims led too often to the fraudulent manufacturing of land-claim documents. Consequently, many legal questions arose as the Anglo lawyers attempted to deal with claims. In 1854, the Office of the Surveyor-General was created to adjudicate Spanish and Mexican land titles.

The Gadsden Purchase Treaty

The Gadsden Purchase Treaty, signed in 1854, was named after James Gadsden who was appointed by the President of the United States to draw up an agreement between the US and Mexico. The purpose of the treaty was to outline in careful detail the acquiring of a new section of land, which the United States wished to purchase from Mexico. The Treaty contained nine articles outlining the exact location of the land, points that required clarification between the Treaty of Guadalupe Hidalgo and the Gadsden Purchase. Article three describes the money to be paid to Mexico. Of the ten million dollars, which was to be paid in New York, seven million would be paid upon signing the treaty and the remaining three million dollars as soon as the boundary line was surveyed, marked and legally established. Care was given to make certain individuals, companies and all concerned would not be negatively affected when traveling along the Colorado River, navigating the Gulf of California or by land travel but at all times respecting the governments of both countries. The Mexican Government agreed to open a port of entry for the railway and in addition a port of Vera Cruz at or near the terminus. The purpose of Article Nine was to outline the need for ratification. The Treaty was drawn up on December 30th, 1853. President Franklin Pierce signed it on the thirtieth of June 1854.

Agriculture

In 1850, the official number of farms in the territory was 3,750. Ten years later that number had almost doubled. Although the Civil War interrupted the growth of farms and the transportation of produce to the markets, the war did help New Mexico increase its cattle raising economy. Soldiers and miners in New Mexico wanted beef. In addition to the needs of soldiers and miners, the government had to feed some 8,500 Indians at Bosque Redondo who were penned up there on a reservation. As it turned out, two Texans—Charles Goodnight and

Oliver Loving were the first to reach the cattle markets with their combined herds and drive them into New Mexico. In some respects this influx of Texans and their herds was just another phase in the Anglo invasion of the state. Within a short time cattle trails criss-crossed the territory in all directions. One of the most famous of New Mexico's early cattle growers was John S. Chisum. His cattle range extended 150 miles, from the Texas border to Fort Sumner and raised about 60,000 head of cattle a year.

Prior to the arrival of the cattlemen, sheep herding dominated the agricultural economy. As early as 1598, Oñate saw that sheep were fully adapted to the semi-arid climate of New Mexico because it was so similar to that of Spain. Some families owned as many as 250,000 head of sheep and enjoyed the large tracts of land they had received as grants from the authorities. Josiah Gregg wrote that there were as many as 500,000 head of sheep exported in one year. With the 1849 gold rush in California another important market for mutton was established.

12

Religious Education in the 19th Century

Cultural heritage reproduces itself and is transmitted from one generation to the next. In primitive societies, the family and tribe or clan manages to do this. Learning takes place by imitation and practice. In more complex societies, formal institutions are entrusted with much of the socialization process. In the 1850s, New Mexico had no public schools so it was the Church that took the responsibility of teaching the young. The Church has always felt that education is incomplete without the knowledge of religion.

With the splendid work the Catholic Church has done over the centuries to bring hope, charity and peace to the unfortunate in virtually every country of the world, the Church has not been without blemish. In our own times we have seen widespread abuse and scandal. During the time of expansion of New Mexico, the Church could not keep up with the needs of the faithful. While still under Mexican control, Santa Fe came under the direction and the responsibility of the Bishop of Durango in Mexico. Supervision and guidance were impossible at that great distance.

Consequently, many men took vows that had no business doing so. Far from serving as positive examples for the settlers, these persons gave the church a terrible reputation. Well documented are instances where these "priests" violated every tenet of their faith. Several were known to have kept mistresses, were heavy gamblers and addicted to alcohol. With the province of New Mexico becoming a territory of the United States, many priests returned to their own country south of the border. Remaining were too few priests, many of whom had strayed from the discipline the cloth.

Old Prayer
(Translated from Spanish)

Like a flock of sheep are we
To the shepherd
Who guides us over
Rocky hilltops.
Pray For Us.

Watched over by Heaven
By Our Holy Father and
The Holy Mother Church
Pray For Us.

Ptotect us from the
Weakness of sin and
Make us strong
Against the Power of Satan
Pray For Us.

Blessed mary, Mother of God
Pray For Us.
Holy Apostles and Martyred Saints
Pray For Us.

13

Jean Baptiste Lamy

On May 21, 1839, two men hurried on foot to catch the coach traveling from their small town in the Massif Central in France to the capital—Paris. This was the first leg of a trip that would take them over thousands of miles. The younger man was Jean Baptiste Lamy. He was twenty-five and had only been ordained six months earlier. His friend was Joseph Priest Machebeuf.

Jean Baptiste's parents were well-to-do peasants. Of their eleven children, only four made it into adulthood. Louis and Baptiste became priests and Marguerite became a nun. As the young men settled in the coach, their thoughts turned to their parents who had not been eager for the young priests to agree on a long ocean voyage to accept a mission in America. After forty-three days crossing the Atlantic, their ship arrived in New York. It was in this manner that the cleric whom we later know as bishop and then archbishop began his career for the Church. He was to bestride religious life in New Mexico like a colossus.

Eleven years after arriving in America, Jean Baptiste Lamy began his trip to the "Great American Desert" traveling from Cincinnati by riverboat. Pius IX had just recently consecrated him to his bishopric. He endured the long processions and hours of sitting, standing and kneeling. On the journey, he began to learn a new language that he knew was essential—Spanish. His travel would take him to New Orleans, Galveston and San Antonio.

Statue of Archbishop J.B. Lamy & St. Francis Cathedral, Santa Fe, NM, ca. 1950 (Courtesy Museum of New Mexico, Neg. #74067), Photo by Tyler Dingee

Early on Sunday, 9 August 1851, Bishop Lamy entered the city of Santa Fe. Paul Horgan writes: "He (Lamy) was astounded to see many thousands advancing (to meet his party) . . . at a point five or six miles from the first houses...most conspicuous in a magnificent carriage was the United States Territorial Governor James Calhoun."

Imagine after such fanfare for his arrival in Santa Fe to be told by the rural vicar—Juan Felipe Ortiz, that Lamy was not the bishop of Santa Fe and would not be recognized as such. Ortiz told Lamy that Santa Fe still reported to the bishop of Durango.

Lamy's first battle then would be to exercise his authority and claim the diocese of New Mexico, which still included all of present-day Arizona. The land mass was larger than his native France. Bishop Lamy met this challenge with stubbornness, perhaps reflecting the character of the people of Auvergne where he was born. Throughout a career, which lasted until 1888, he took on huge battles and had the drive to bring them to successful conclusions.

Bishop Lamy had three main goals for New Mexico. First, he would bring education to Santa Fe. During his first weeks in Santa Fe he realized how important education would be to the people. Education, not just book knowledge, he insisted, but education in Christian amenity. He wrote: "The state of immorality in matters of sex is so deplorable that the most urgent need is to open schools for girls under the direction of Sisters of Charity." He had already been looking for a site to build a convent. As for boys, Lamy wanted a school for them in every parish. Davis writes of the state of education in New Mexico in 1856: "The standard of education in New Mexico is at a very low ebb, and there is a larger number of persons who cannot read and write than in any other Territory in the Union. The census of 1850 shows a population of 61,547 inhabitants, of whom 25,089 are returned as being able to read and write . . . the number attending school is given as 460, which is about one scholar to every one hundred and twenty-five inhabitants."

Secondly, Lamy would build a cathedral dedicated to the Patron Saint of Santa Fe—Saint Francis. This cathedral would not be made of adobe but of sandstone, quarried locally. It would have stained glass windows imported from France. La Parroquia, the church, which was to be replaced by the cathedral, had been built in 1710-12 and served as the main house of worship until the arrival of the bishop. Only the chapel which houses the statue of the Conquistadora, remains today from La Parroquia. For his great cathedral, Lamy recruited the architects Antoine and Projectus Mouly, father and son, from France and stonemasons from France and Italy. The Moulys knew the medieval Romanesque of southern France well. Historian John Kessell commented on this: "It is fashionable in our day to berate Lamy and his Frenchmen for their callous disregard of Pueblo and Hispanic

76

culture in general and of indigenous architecture in particular. But conquest is like that."

La Parroquia, Santa Fe, NM, ca.1867 (Courtesy Museum of New Mexico, Neg. #55484), Photo by Nicholas Brown

Perhaps it was not conquest that prompted Lamy's decision but rather a deep dislike for the adobe brick which he considered inferior to stone and less permanent.

Thirdly, Bishop Lamy would bring order to the religious ranks of Santa Fe. He would reform this holy establishment, which had been allowed to grow stagnant and corrupt. He would remove priests from their posts and unfrock them, some from members of New Mexico's leading families, causing politicians to attempt to oust him. One priest who shocked Bishop Lamy because of an undisciplined lifestyle was Padre Gallegos who lived openly with his mistress. Bishop Lamy excommunicated him. This had little effect on the priest who immediately went to join the Episcopal Church and then later went into politics, which may have been his true calling. The Santa cafe is located on the site today where Padre Gallegos's house once stood. The building is an example of Territorial Revival Style—a euphemism for a mixture of forms.

In 1859, Lamy wrote to the Society at Paris to say he was sending Father Peter Eguillon, his vicar, to France to find more priests and to enlist members of the order of Christian Brothers for the purpose of establishing a permanent school for boys.

In addition to ten priests, Father Eguillon was able to enlist four members of the Christian Brothers—Hilarien, Gondulph, Geramius and Galmier Joseph.

They left Le Havre, France on August 17th and completed the sea voyage in fourteen days. For a total of two months, the party of priests and brothers traveled by various means of transportation on their way to New Mexico. Bishop Lamy's plan was not only to build a school for boys but also a school for girls. In September 1851, he wrote to his old friend Bishop Purcell: "The Sisters of Notre Dame will receive a letter from me . . . I have asked if they could send me a few Sisters to establish a good school . . . or if it was not in their power to spare any Sisters, will you please write to Emmitsburgh to obtain three or four Sisters of Charity . . . or Sisters of any order."

To meet the needs of Bishop Lamy, six Sisters of Loretto were appointed to Santa Fe. They were Sisters Matilda Mills, superior, Catherine Mahoney, Magdalen Hayden, Rosanna Dant, Monica Bailey and Roberta Brown. Only four of the original six reached Santa Fe. Mother Superior Mills died of cholera and Sister Monica turned back because of illness of the same disease but traveled to Santa Fe three years later.

The legacy of Archbishop Lamy is considerable: "Through his (Lamy's) efforts, Santa Fe today has St. Vincent Hospital, established by the Sisters of Charity; St. Francis Cathedral . . . Loretto Chapel, also built in the French style for the Sisters of Loretto and their institution, Loretto Academy for Girls; and St. Michael's College."

It was on June 16, 1896 that St. Vincent's Sanatorium burned down. *The New Mexican* reported the incident: "The burning of St. Vincent Sanatorium in this city, on Sunday evening, is not only a serious loss to the noble order of Sisters of Charity, but it is a loss of no slight magnitude to the city of Santa Fe. It is the pioneer institution of the kind in the far west."

The importance of that institution cannot be overemphasized. Richard Harris writes: ". . . physicians came to recognize that the high, dry, mild climate was ideal for alleviating the symptoms of lung disease . . . first the church-owned St. Vincent's Sanatorium and later the renowned Sunmount Sanitarium filled to capacity with refugees from the coal-smoke pollution of the eastern industrial cities, seeking a cure for tuberculosis and other chronic respiratory illnesses."

It may be of interest to note that the selection of a French-born bishop for Santa Fe may not have been casual. It may very well have been an attempt by the Church to bring some balance to the prevailing Spanish/Mexican influence in the Church. In addition to replacing an adobe church with a Romanesque cathedral, he modeled the Loretto Chapel on the Sainte Chapelle in Paris.

The Loretto Chapel and Academy

It was Projectus Mouly, son of the architect of the cathedral, who undertook the Loretto Chapel. It was a serious responsibility for a youth of eighteen, especially in that his father could not give him guidance. Antoine Mouly was going blind and had to be returned to France. The Chapel is a success in every way. It is today the oldest Gothic structure west of the Mississippi.

Loretto Chapel, College Street, Santa Fe, NM, ca. 1880 (Courtesy Museum of New Mexico, Neg. #76953)

SISTERS' CHAPEL, FROM RIO CHIQUITO.

Much has already been written about the spiral staircase. In deference to our readers who know little about the Loretto Chapel and for those who may come to Santa Fe for the purpose of seeing the Chapel, we might say a few words about the staircase.

There is a legend and like most legends, this one varies greatly. It seems that the Chapel of Our Lady of Light, called today "The Loretto Chapel" was completed in 1878 but to the dismay of the Sisters, there was no way to access the choir loft. One version tells of a rope ladder that was put into place but it was naturally unacceptable to the Sisters. Since prayer was their way of life, they prayed to St. Joseph, father of Jesus and patron saint of carpenters for a solution to their problem. On the last day of their novena a white-bearded man arrived with a few basic tools and asked for work as a carpenter.

He was immediately put to work to build a staircase. He worked swiftly and masterfully making a spiral staircase made up of two 360-degree turns leading to the choir loft. Having finished, the man disappeared without being paid for his work. The Sisters believed that it was St. Joseph himself who came to their aid. Mary J. Straw Cook devotes some effort to give the historical account of this legend. Her book is entitled, *Loretto*.

It should be noted that another church existed at the site of the present Plaza Galeria at 66 West San Francisco. It was called La Castrense, or La Capilla de Nuestra Senora de la Luz. This was a Mexican Baroque-style military church, which fronted the plaza from 1760 to 1859. It fell into disrepair and Bishop Lamy ordered it demolished.

Although Archbishop Lamy lived to a ripe old age and died in February 1888, having traveled thousands of miles to fulfill his mission to New Mexico, he was erroneously reported to have been killed in July of 1867.

Not many of us are given the opportunity to read our own obituary. Page four of the *New York Herald* on July 19th reported the following: "A train was captured last Sunday, near Fort Larned, by the Indians. Bishop Lamy, ten priests and six Sisters of Charity accompanied the train as passengers en route to Santa Fe. The men were killed, scalped and shockingly mutilated. The females were carried away captives. This information comes through reliable sources."

St. Michael's School for Boys

The original four Christian Brothers labored under harsh conditions during the first years of the school. The Brothers taught in an adobe hut close to St. Michael's Church in the Analco section of the city. The school received its charter in 1874. Continuing in the tradition of St. John Baptist de la Salle, the school flourished. About the time the Loretto Chapel was being dedicated, the Christian Brothers began to demolish their old adobe school on College Street and would lay the cornerstone for a two-story building with a third floor incorporated in the mansard. In 1947 the school moved from the center of the city to the newly acquired Bruns Army Hospital, which allowed space for its growth.

In 1966, the Institution changed its name to the "College of Santa Fe." Such individuals as Brother Benildus, Brother Raymond Ogden, Brother Cyprian Luke, Brother Donald Mouton and Dr. James Fries are synonymous with its growth, enlightenment and dedication. Under five previous presidents the college has grown in size, complexity and reputation. At this writing, the College of Santa Fe has its sixth president, Dr. Linda N. Hanson and is thriving under her expert guidance.

San Miguel Chapel and College, Santa Fe, NM, ca. 1885 (Courtesy Museum of New Mexico, Neg. #10076)

Federal Courthouse

In 1853, as part of a plan to render the architecture of Santa Fe more harmonious with the rest of the United States and thereby make the territory more acceptable for statehood, a building was constructed to serve as the Territorial Capitol. With only twenty thousand dollars, the project was begun with an additional fifty thousand dollars added for the increased costs. Unfortunately, the money could only construct the walls. This structure, built in the Greek Revival Style, remained without a roof for thirty years and never served as the territorial capitol. A temporary roof was added in 1883 but the building was not completed until 1930. It serves quite well today as the Federal Courthouse.

It was also in 1883 that Santa Fe celebrated its Tertio-Millennial Celebration. Clearly, the city was in the mood for a big fiesta so the enthusiasts arbitrarily selected the year of 1550 as the beginning of the Spanish occupation of the city. (Actually, it was not until the arrival of Peralta in 1609-10 that this took place). The city planners then calculated that the city was 333 years old or one third of a century. That is how they got the name of "Tertio-Millennial." With the construction of the road surrounding the federal courthouse called the "Federal Oval," used conveniently for horse racing and much later for high school track meets, the area became popular for picnics.

Buffalo Soldiers

Blacks fought in George Washington's army during the War of Independence and in every war since then. The first black regiment in the United States fought under Colonel Higginson in 1861 with the South Carolina Volunteers. Five years later an Act of Congress authorized six regiments of Black troops—two of cavalry and four of infantry. It was September 1866 that the 9th Cavalry Regiment was activated at Greenville, Louisiana. The men carried out their work with older horses and substandard equipment. Often they were housed in run-down forts. They accomplished the tasks given to them, however, extremely well and earned the respect of all those who saw them fight. The 9th was transferred to the District of New Mexico during the winter and spring of 1875-76 and spent the next six years fighting the Apaches.

14

The Civil War

In principle, the plan had merit. Texas, living outside the nation it had wished to join thirty years earlier, was ready to spearhead an invasion of New Mexico. Not only did Texas plan to take for itself all the land east of the Rio Grande River but also thought its troops could run through Colorado and cut west to California and seize the gold mines. This was a bold plan but if successful might have added considerable real estate for the Confederacy. In July 1861, confederate soldiers invaded New Mexico Territory. The battle lasted only twelve months.

Lt. Col. John R. Baylor led his Confederate forces and succeeded in capturing Albuquerque and Santa Fe. The taking of these two cities was quite an easy operation. A New Orleans newspaper carried the following: "In February, 1861, Colonel John R. Baylor organized the Fourth regiment of Texas cavalry and with a battalion of six companies marched from San Antonio to El Paso, Texas, capturing forts on the line of march which had been vacated by Union troops . . . from there the battalion proceeded to New Mexico and captured Fort Fillmore."

These Texans, before leaving San Antonio had seized the US arsenal and barracks. The Civil War was moving to New Mexico. Secretary of War, Simon Cameron, acknowledged that New Mexico was in no condition to resist an attack. The regular troops had been sent out of the territory to fight on other fronts. Most of the soldiers were disgruntled, not having received any pay for some time. Because of the long-extended drought in New Mexico, there was little grass for horses to feed on which made sending cavalry regiments senseless.

On July 8th, General H.H. Sibley was given the task by Confederate President Davis to drive the federal forces out of New Mexico. He knew the country. It has been speculated that Sibley may have considered the task below him and that he would have preferred to remain in Virginia or go on to Gettysburg for an important campaign. He did not take his task very seriously, partly because he thought the Southwest would be handed to him on a silver platter because of the sympathizers for the confederate cause. He may not have taken the precautions that Colonel Baylor may have taken.

The Battles of Valverde and Glorieta

The first major battle of the Civil War in New Mexico was fought at Valverde on February 21, 1862. Commanding the Union forces was Edward R.S. Canby. As often was the case in the Civil War in which brother was sometimes pitted against brother, Henry Sibley and Edward Canby had been close friends, having been to West Point together. The battle of Valverde was a victory for Sibley's troops during which they destroyed a battery of Union artillery forces. Canby dug in at Fort Craig with more than three thousand men so the Texas soldiers bypassed the fort.

The confederate forces then marched up the Rio Grande. On March 2, 1862, the confederate flag was raised over Albuquerque after both sides agreed to curtail hostilities and save the city from destruction. The Confederate troops lost no time taking Santa Fe and raising its flag—the fourth flag: Spanish, Mexican, Territorial and now Confederate to fly above the Palace of the Governors. By most accounts the war in New Mexico should have ended at that time. The Union forces were seriously outnumbered, six hundred Union forces against over a thousand Confederate forces.

The Battle of Glorieta was going badly for the Union Army. The immediate aim of the Confederate forces was to take Fort Union and then go north into Colorado. In a brilliant move, Chaves of the Colorado Volunteers led Major Chivington's group over rugged terrain behind enemy lines and destroyed a supply train of more than sixty wagons and killed about a thousand mules. Without food, arms and other supplies, the Confederate army could not continue to fight so they beat a quick retreat down the Rio Grande.

At Peralta, just south of Albuquerque, the third battle of the Civil War was fought. Canby and his soldiers, angered at having been forced by the powerful and fully-equipped Confederate army to seek refuge in Fort Craig, were spoiling for a battle. It was more of a chase than a battle. The Rebels were heading toward El Paso with Canby's men on their heels.

The Rebels sued for a truce and buried their dead, thus ending the war in New Mexico. In about a year of fighting, about thirteen hundred men were killed with no territorial gains for the Confederate Army. For his part in the victory at Glorieta, John Chivington was promoted to colonel. He remained with the Colorado Volunteers for the rest of the war and led the infamous and controversial attack on Black Kettle at Sand Creek in November 1864. He was pilloried in the press for his brutality.

On the Confederate side, Henry Sibley left the country after the war and tried to help the Khedive of Egypt organize an army. His attempts were unsuccessful due to mismanagement and his continuing penchant for the bottle. Finally he returned to Fredericksburg, Virginia where he died penniless in 1886.

The Battle of Glorieta is sometimes called the "Gettysburg of the West" because it was a decisive battle of the Civil War

As a footnote to the Civil War, Santa Feans enjoy an old square called "Sena Plaza." Jose Sena, a major on the side of the Union forces during the Civil War, inherited this property from his mother. Ownership goes back to the time when Don Diego de Vargas gave the property as a land grant to Captain Arias de Quiros. Jose Sena expanded the property from a small house to a very large thirty-three-room hacienda, to house twenty-three children. Originally the ground floor had no openings to the streets except a large wagon passageway on the north side of the plaza. Today it is a popular meeting place for dining and listening to music.

In 1870, a territorial governor who had scant visibility or success in his functions as the chief civil administrator of New Mexico decided to enter the history books by reason of stupidity. William Pile sold the Spanish archives stored in the Palace of the Governors as scrap paper, destroying most of the documents from the Spanish Colonial and Mexican periods. Aside from the burning of the territorial capitol much later, this act by Pile has hampered and frustrated much scholarship on the history of New Mexico.

Kit Carson

Of all the mountain men who came to New Mexico, Kit Carson had the most impact on the future of the territory. Christopher Houston Carson was born in 1809, on Christmas Eve in Kentucky. Chris lost his father when he was only nine years old and for lack of money, Chris had to drop out of school. To earn money, he learned the trade of saddle making. At the first opportunity, the boy joined a wagon train that was going to Santa Fe.

During the next few years, Kit Carson lived part of the time in Taos and spent part of his time fur trapping throughout the West. In the 1840s, he worked for a while as a hunter for William Bent at Bent's Fort. He became fluent in Indian languages and integrated himself fully into the world of the Indian. His first two wives were Arapaho and Cheyenne.

During the war in New Mexico, the Comanches, Apaches and Navajos made trouble by raiding the settlements. Both sides claimed the other had broken the truce. In September 1862, General James Carleton succeeded Canby as commander of the Military Department. He made plans for solving the Indian problem. The Mescalero Apaches were to be dealt with first. Carleton engaged Colonel Kit Carson to move about four hundred warriors and their families to Bosque

Redondo in the valley of the Pecos River where they were to be held until decisions could be made about their future. The troops at Fort Sumner were to guard the Apaches.

The Navajo question was more complex. The peaceful Navajos were to be separated from the hostile ones. Those who would be willing to be separated were sent to Bosque Redondo. Carleton met with the Navajo leaders and told them their word had been broken too many times and that the army would use force to control them. Kit Carson had the unpleasant task of going to Canyon de Chelly to show the Navajos the army meant business. Carson was opposed to the demand for unconditional surrender of the Navajos or they were to face extermination. He attempted to be relieved of his duties but was unsuccessful. The hostile Navajos would not cooperate and would not surrender. It was in the last months of 1863 that Carson's troops marched through the Navajo homeland. Their mission was to destroy

all Navajo sources of food supply—their crops and stores were burned, fruit trees destroyed and livestock captured. The starving Indians were at last willing to comply with the demands of General Carleton—obey rather than be put to death. Carson led the

Colonel Christopher "Kit" Carson, St. Louis, Missouri, December 1864 (Courtesy Museum of New Mexico, Neg. #7151)

Navajos to the reservation at Bosque Redondo. The Navajos refer to this displacement at the "Long Walk."

The Bosque Redondo project was doomed for failure. The Apaches and Navajos were not compatible. The hope that the tribes would soon become self-sufficient was, as well, unrealized. Soon afterward, the Navajos were allowed to return to their homeland; the Apache broke away and disappeared into the hills.

The sentiments of the people of Santa Fe are reflected in the following: "The success of Col. Carson will distinguish him and those with him. They deserve and will receive the gratitude of the people, for every Indian they have killed or made captive. Go on gallant, Kit, says New Mexico, and wipe out the hostile Indians."

After the Civil War, the territory and its capital, Santa Fe suffered a period of general lawlessness. In one month, three murders were committed near the plaza in addition to countless beatings. Few men were willing to risk their lives to become sheriffs or deputies. Soldiers of the cavalry were spending more time chasing thieves than in fighting Indians. Beck speaks of a case of political assassination in Santa Fe: "One notorious example was the slaying of John P. Slough, Chief Justice of the Territorial Supreme Court. Slough, who originally arrived in New Mexico with the Colorado Volunteers during the Civil War, was shot down in La Fonda Hotel in 1867 by William L. Rynerson on the pretext that the judge had reached for his derringer first."

Lawlessness existed in the Southwest for several reasons. There was little homogeneity among the citizens who traveled to Santa Fe after New Mexico became a Mexican province in 1821.The law that applied there was not made for the conditions that existed and was unsuitable for those conditions. Since it was perceived that no one could enforce the law, each man had to make his own law and usually he enforced it with his six-shooter. In the absence of law in the social conditions that prevailed, men worked out an extra-legal code that demanded fair play. For example, one must never shoot an adversary in the back or shoot an unarmed man.

In addition to crime, the citizens had grown careless with disposing of their garbage. Water Street today was once an open sewer where dead animals and refuse of every sort floated. The police posted a ruling, which read: "Every house owner or head of family within the limits of the city of Santa Fe shall specially take care that his servants or attendants do not throw dirty water, rubbish, ashes or kitchen offal in the public squares, roads, streets or lanes of the City."

15

The Railroad

Although there was some ambivalence concerning the coming of the railroad to New Mexico, most of the population viewed it with excited anticipation. It meant more tourism and more trade which meant more prosperity. The traditionalists were concerned that the railroad would bring an undesirable element of society. In the 1870s, as the railroad began to cross Kansas, the fervor grew. The Santa Fe Trail had been the only connection with the East and trade had been brisk. After the end of the Civil War, there were fewer problems with the Indians. The Trail was carrying unprecedented weight in goods, much of it military cargo for the new forts. The railroad promised to increase the capacity a hundred fold. *The New Mexican* cautioned its readers: "The citizens of Santa Fe must themselves show some measure of confidence in the city if they expect railroads and manufactures and commercial men to show confidence in a town and come here and invest their capital."

The commercial entities of Santa Fe were urged to raise money to support the coming railroad. The railroad companies expected established communities to subsidize the construction of its lines. After all, it would be these communities that would benefit financially from the increased trade. Initially, Santa Fe reacted badly to the proposal that it had to help pay for the railroad. Agents from the Denver and Rio Grande Railroad were sent packing. Clearly the leading citizens had to get used to the idea.

Another problem that was unforeseen earlier was the fact that the railroads had had a relatively easy time crossing the plains of Kansas. When the railroad made it into Colorado, especially the mountains around Raton Pass, the owners saw that each mile in rough terrain would cost many additional dollars.

City leaders, fearing that Santa Fe might be bypassed altogether by the railroad, made contact with the Atchison, Topeka and Santa Fe (AT&SF) Company. Meanwhile, the engineers projecting the path of the railroad advised that Santa Fe be bypassed altogether. Their reasons were sound—to leave the flat land to bring the railroad to an altitude of seven thousand feet just to include the capital of New Mexico made no sense. The residents of Santa Fe were disappointed. At last a bond issue was approved for $150,000 to have an eighteen-mile spur line join Santa Fe to the main line at a town named after the Archbishop, "Lamy." The first train arrived in Santa Fe in April, 1880; it was an excursion train for celebrating the opening of a new era.

The labor force on the railroad was at first mainly Irish. Soon New Mexicans were hired and even some Indians. All along the line, new towns began springing up. Opportunity arose for those who wanted to prepare food for the passengers at the various stops.

Las Vegas, NM was one of the first towns to benefit from the arrival of the railroad in 1879. The city shipped out in one year ten million dollars worth of hides, wool and pelts. The AT&SF started to build hotels along its line. In Santa Fe, the location where La Fonda presently stands was the Exchange Hotel—an establishment for clients of the railway. One story relates that Billy the Kid once washed dishes in the Exchange Hotel.

In 1919, the Exchange Hotel was demolished. The present-day La Fonda was built a year later on the same site. In 1926, La Fonda became a part of the Harvey House hotel chain and remained one for more than forty years.

The railroad permitted the transportation of heavy machinery, which allowed more lumber and stone to be processed locally. Railroad companies energetically promoted settlement along the western routes, luring prospective homesteaders with pictures of bountiful fields, prosperous farmers and easy rewards.

The black community of Nicodemus, Kansas owed its existence to such boosterism. Handbills were distributed that said: "All Colored People that want to go TO KANSAS, on September 5, 1877, can do so for $5.00."

The railroad was allowing the West to be populated. The Homestead Act of 1862 gave impetus to this movement. The Homestead Act with its amendments increased the size of a land grant from 160 acres to 640 acres and a shortened period of compulsory residence.

The stagecoach robbers of the Santa Fe Trail naturally mutated into train robbers in the 1880s. In a small New Mexican town, the following sign was posted near the railroad station: "Notice to Thieves, Thugs, Fakirs and Bunkosteerers: If found within the limits of this city after Ten O'clock PM, this night, you will be invited to attend a Grand Neck-Tie Party, the expense of which will be borne by 100 SUBSTANTIAL CITIZENS."

Robbing passengers on rail coaches succeeded only part of the time. In the annals of the railway, most robbers were either shot in the act or jailed when the train reached the next depot.

16

Governor Lew Wallace

The man who was to become the 97th governor since Western colonization, Lew Wallace, was unique. He was the son of an Indiana governor, an ex-Civil War hero and an author of a successful novel about the life of Jesus Christ—*Ben-Hur*. Besides having a building and a school named after him, he is today relatively unknown. In his time, however, he was very popular. His published books earned him more royalties that any American novelist before him. Author William Barrett compares the concerns of the 21st century governor to those of the 1880s. He says: "Present-day New Mexico has high crime, not enough prisons, Indian conflicts and an activist Republican governor warring with legislators and judges. Just like back in 1880."

When Wallace arrived in Santa Fe, he already knew his priority would be law and order. There was a run of crimes that was quite serious—murder of prominent citizens, rape and grand theft.

The Lincoln County War was mistakenly labeled a range war—involving disputes of the cattle market but in truth it was a blood feud. Billy the Kid got involved on the side of one of the factions and drew so much attention that Governor Wallace went to Lincoln County in southern New Mexico to investigate the situation. On the surface, Wallace saw an attempt on one side to eliminate a competitor for the beef market. It was Alexander McSween who bought an interest in a ranch and built a store to challenge Lawrence Murphy's trade monopoly. On the side of McSween was an Englishman named John Henry Tunstall. In the first volley of the Lincoln County War, Tunstall was gunned down in cold blood. Enter William Bonney, later to be called "Billy the Kid," and taking the side of the dead Tunstall, he had the two gunmen responsible for the killing, murdered.

New Mexico Territorial Governor Lew Wallace (1827-1905) (Courtesy Museum of New Mexico, Neg. #15295)

It was in the midst of this convoluted situation that Governor Wallace found himself. In order to get sufficient information, Wallace negotiated personally with and promised clemency to, the murderer, Billy the Kid. The deal, however, fell through and Billy the Kid was convicted of murder. According to notes taken from the meeting, the following conversation took place between Governor Wallace and Billy the Kid:

"You don't look at all as I had pictured you. Here you are a clean-cut good-looking youth of nineteen. But I've heard stories about you... I am old enough to be your father. So Billy, I am going to talk to you as a father."

The Kid nodded.

"I have come all this way to Lincoln for the special purpose of persuading you to stop fighting. I have faith you can help me. You see President Hayes has sent me to New Mexico to establish peace . . ."

"I couldn't if I tried . . ." answered the Kid.

In the course of his tenure as governor, Wallace had his share of problems with the legislature. Wallace lent his support to Eugene Fiske to be the attorney general but the legislature refused to confirm. Not wanting to be denied, Wallace waited for the legislature to adjourn and then appointed Fiske. In 1881, the opponents went to court and the ruling came out against Wallace.

Governor Wallace grew disillusioned with his work and in March 1881, he approached the new President Garfield and submitted his resignation. On leaving his post, he said to a group of friends: "At least I haven't been jailed or murdered like some of my predecessors."

Before leaving New Mexico, in a letter to his wife he wrote: "I have spent enough time in this place. There is nobody who cares for me and nobody I care for."

Susan Wallace, the governor's wife is quoted as saying: "We should have another war with Old Mexico to make her take back New Mexico."

17

Billy the Kid

No attempt will be made here to go into any depth about Billy the Kid or to offer opinions as to what constitutes fact or legend. It's unfortunate that the only photograph of him that is available to us makes him out to be less of a hero than our imagination might require. In the photo, he is standing with his rifle at his side. He appears to be narrow at the shoulder and wide at the hips and his face appears to be irregularly shaped. We know that he had several names: "Henry McCarty," "William H. Bonney" and "The Kid."

His parents were Catherine and Michael McCarty—immigrants from poverty-stricken Ireland and its famine. When Billy's mother died of tuberculosis about nine years after she had married Billy's stepfather, the boy was pretty much on his own. At fourteen, he fell in with a rough element, did odd jobs and learned how to steal for a living.

In front of witnesses in a saloon in Fort Grant, Arizona Territory, Billy killed his first person (at least that we know of). In an argument with a blacksmith named "Cahill", Billy drew his pistol and shot the man dead. He was an outlaw at seventeen.

It is here we join the story we began earlier in speaking about Governor Wallace. Billy served as a ranch hand for a wealthy Englishman—John Henry Tunstall. When Tunstall was killed, Billy and his gang called the "Regulators" killed the two men responsible for Tunstall's death.

"The Finale—The Kid Killed by the Sheriff at Fort Sumner," New Mexico, July 14, 1881 (Courtesy Museum of New Mexico, Neg. #47640)

From 1878-1880, Billy was in Fort Sumner. He had been rustling cattle and had managed to remain on the loose. Billy was wanted for the killing of Sheriff Brady as well. During the Lincoln War he added two more notches to his gun. Pat Garrett, the sheriff of Lincoln County vowed to capture the Kid.

Garrett captured Billy in December 1880; two of Billy's sidekicks were shot. Billy's attitude was such that he believed he was invincible. He was tried in Mesilla and convicted of several murders and sentenced to hang. The Kid was being held in a second-story room of the courthouse. He was one month away from being hanged. On April 18, 1881, Billy escaped by killing his two guards. Billy left Lincoln and went to Fort Sumner and hid for a couple of months. On July 14th, Garrett located the fugitive and shot him in the heart. Billy the Kid was twenty-one years old and had twenty-one notches in his gun.

Two stories about Billy place him in Santa Fe—one as a dishwasher at the hotel now called La Fonda, the other as he was being pursued by the posse down the road Agua Fria. As a footnote of history, Garrett was shot and killed by Wayne Brazil over a lease on Garrett's ranch that Brazil held. The year was 1908.

Geronimo's Surrender

Lionel A. Sheldon succeeded Lew Wallace as governor of New Mexico in 1881. Among his concerns, which were many, was the Apache Indian problem. In May of 1885, the last year of Sheldon's tenure as governor, the Apaches fled the San Carlos reservation in Arizona. Under the leadership of Mangus Chihuahua and the shaman Geronimo, the "hostiles" headed for the open spaces, which were so dear to the semi-nomad people.

Life on the reservation had been difficult and confining for the Apaches. If the nature of the Apaches had been to live and let live, the history of this people would have been written differently. The Apaches, however, were warlike and wreaked destruction in their path. The band consisted of thirty-five men, eight boys and one hundred and one women and children. Over a period of sixteen months, they would remain free while five thousand troops and many Indian auxiliaries would try to round them up. During that time, the Apaches killed seventy-five citizens and several officers and soldiers of the regular army.

General Crook established a command post in Fort Bayard, New Mexico. After months of rumors of the whereabouts of the hostiles, months of indignant telegrams with Washington, the army was closing in on Geronimo. In mid-July of 1886, Lt. Charles Gatewood crossed into Mexico from New Mexico. More than a month later, he picked up the trail of the Apaches. He met the hostiles on the banks of the Bavispe River and urged them to surrender. On September 3rd, Geronimo and his followers agreed to terms and were taken into custody.

18

Education and Growth in the 19th Century

With the impetus given by Archbishop Lamy for the establishment of a school for boys under the Christian Brothers and a school for girls under the Sisters of Loretto and the Sisters of Charity, there was a continued growth of church-sponsored education during the rest of the century throughout the state.

The Jesuits established St. Mary's School in Albuquerque in 1893, which was run as a coeducational parochial institution. St. Catherine's Industrial Indian School of Santa Fe was founded in 1886 by the Archbishop Salpointe and Mother Catherine Drexel of Philadelphia. In 1888, the Christian Brothers founded the La Salle Institute at Las Vegas, New Mexico and maintained it until 1927.

Protestant groups were also active in developing schools in the mid-1800s. The Presbyterian Church established a day school at Laguna Pueblo in 1866. Under Reverend Harwood, the Methodist Church made its first steps in education in 1871. The Congregational Church came to Santa Fe in 1878.

With illiteracy marked at over seventy-five percent, there were early attempts to create free public schools. It was not until 1891 that a law was passed to provide for a Territorial Board of Education. A tax levy was put into place with the proceeds given to the districts.

Attendance at school became mandatory between the ages of eight and sixteen for a minimum of three months per year.

Somewhat later, the problems of bilingual instruction in public schools were reduced. As employment opportunities grew and travel outside the state became more common, New Mexicans had more contact with Anglo populations and were able to learn to improve their knowledge of English.

In 1892, higher education came to New Mexico. The Territorial Legislature established several schools. The University of New Mexico began its classes in Albuquerque.

Thomas B. Catron

One of the first US Senators for New Mexico was a Republican—Thomas B. Catron who arrived in New Mexico in 1866 after serving in the Confederate Army. "Boss" Catron was determined to make himself rich. As a lawyer, he dedicated himself to the complicated business of sorting out the land grant problems. As an expert on land grants, he made a fortune for himself and managed to acquire vast expanses of land. He was a director and major shareholder in cattle corporations that owned the southern half of Santa Fe County as well as most of what is now Catron County. At one time or another, he gained an interest or clear title in 34 land grants, totaling three million acres. A good many of the people he represented were illiterate and could not read the documents he placed before them. He was accused of being unprofessional and corrupt but he was too clever to suffer from these accusations.

As a politician, he practically ran the Republican Party single-handedly. He was the acknowledged leader of the Santa Fe Ring—a group of hard-line politically astute businessmen. With the appointment of Miguel Otero, Jr., as territorial governor in 1897, Catron's power began to diminish. Men such as Catron grew rich through tactics that would be illegal today but this was widespread in the American West during the "Robber Baron" era.

Miguel Antonio Otero, Jr.

Miguel Antonio Otero, Jr. was born in St. Louis, Missouri, October 17, 1849. His parents returned to their permanent home in New Mexico when the boy was two years old. He received a religious education at a local school—Notre Dame. His first job was that of a bookkeeper and he entered politics in 1883 as City Treasurer of Las Vegas. After working in several clerk positions in various court offices, he got involved with the Republican Party and was appointed Territorial Governor in 1897.

Junketing senators, ostensibly to gather positive information about New Mexico in its continued bid for statehood, would instead cement their preconceived opinions and gather negative data. Miguel Otero described such an activity: "He (L. G. Rothschild) would sneak around the slum districts and meet impossible people in order to make an adverse report on conditions as found by him. Absolutely not the slightest attention was paid to the favorable side of the territory, and no inquiry was made covering education, industry, manufacturing, banking, stock-raising, mining or farming."

In a sense, the Spanish-American War helped New Mexico in its quest for statehood. In 1898, Congress declared war against Spain in an attempt to help Cuba win its independence from that country. The question asked was whether New Mexico would join in the fight against its first mother country. The response was resoundingly affirmative. The war had a short duration—six months and the United States achieved its aims. New Mexico had, at that time, the first Hispanic governor since 1846—Miguel Antonio Otero, Jr. Governor Otero also had the distinction of serving the longest period as part of the United States. With the outbreak of the war, the governor called for volunteers and the response was overwhelming.

His father Miguel Antonio Otero was a major contributor to the economic development of New Mexico. He was seated as a Territorial Delegate to the U.S. House of Representatives in 1856 and with the support of Bishop Lamy was reelected to the next two congresses. When Otero senior completed his terms in congress, he was considered for the post of Minister to Spain. President Lincoln believed Otero was exceptionally qualified. Otero, however, declined the office.

New Mexico Territorial Governor Miguel Antonio Otero, Jr.
(Courtesy Museum of New Mexico, Neg. #50608)

19

Lifestyle in the 19th Century

With the Santa Fe Trail and later with the railroads, Anglo-Americans flooded into New Mexico. Their initial appraisal was at first uniformly negative. They had stepped back in time and had found none of the modern conveniences they were used to and thought they needed. Much of what was prevalent in sixteenth century Spain still existed in nineteenth century New Mexico. The society included a few very wealthy people but most of the people had to struggle for an existence. The Church had as much a hold on its congregation as it did in Medieval Europe. Santa Fe, the territorial capital, failed to impress the visitors. The roads were poorly maintained, the houses were constructed with any materials that could be found. There seemed to be little order in the life of the inhabitants.

Those visitors who had heard about the Palace of the Governors before coming to Santa Fe were exceptionally disappointed by the long, low-slung building, constructed it seemed from the very mud of the narrow lanes that surrounded it. The "puddle adobe"—the simple way the Indians had poured wet mud and waited for it to dry before pouring more—was improved upon by the Spaniards who taught the Indians how to form bricks and stack the walls of their houses.

Visitors in the nineteenth century saw that little change had taken place in this construction since the conquistadors. The houses were built, as many had been built in Spain, with a small patio in the middle of the area with several rooms opening to the patio. No openings were placed on the outside of the house, for reasons of security. For the most part, floors were of earth, sometimes treated to give them a hardened surface. The roofs were flat and could not prevent the rain from coming into the rooms.

Usually one room had a fireplace lit at a time. This was often the kitchen where the family gathered to eat and do whatever chores they could. The bedrooms were not heated. The bedding was heated with hot coals prior to turning in for the night. Candles were made at home and used sparingly. Similar to the custom in Spain, women used a lime and chalk mixture to cover the walls making them white. This surface did not last long and, as a rule, had to be redone every year.

Furniture was sparse, even among the wealthy. Beds were rare, only mattresses were thrown on the floor at night. These mattresses were stuffed with straw and often some sweet-smelling herbs. Valuables were kept in trunks, usually made of rawhide. Kitchen utensils were usually made of earthenware and had multiple uses during the meal.

New Mexicans wore clothing that provided warmth and did not change as often as we, in this century, would prefer. Clothing was homemade with close-fitting buckskin to keep out the cold. Scents were used by the women to compensate for and cover up odors that came from fireplace smoke and perspiration. Despite the poverty in which most of the people lived, there was that pride in appearance for the men and a bit of the coquette in the women. The women would wear a "rebozo"—a long scarf up to six feet long that was thrown over the shoulders and dangled to the waist. It served as a bonnet, a shawl, an apron and a bodice. Men wore their "sombrero," a word that comes from the Spanish word of "sombra "meaning "shade." An all-purpose garment for the men was the serape, which was slung over the shoulders and could serve as an overcoat, raincoat or blanket.

With the permission of the Church, dances were frequently held on fiesta days. Sponsored often by the Church, these dances were carefully monitored. The instruments that accompanied the dance were the violin and the guitar. A good deal of thumping was a sign that the dance was unusually successful. The strict behavior of the New Mexican was sometimes disturbed by the arrival of the Anglo who liked to drink alcohol at the dances.

Despite the prohibition of the friars, gambling was ever-present in New Mexico. Horse racing and cock fighting were common and betting always made the action interesting. At one time, Santa Fe had sixty licensed gambling places. With the coming of the soldiers and the building of Fort Marcy, gambling reached its peak.

While the Puritans of the East of an earlier period were restrained in matters of sex, available records show that premarital sex in New Mexico was widely tolerated in the 19th century but marital infidelities were severely punished. The Church, of course, strongly forbade this behavior.

Also sponsored by the Catholic Church were the plays that depicted the important moments in the lives of Christ and the Virgin Mary. These plays were often held on the grounds of the church and performed during the holy days. Because the people were predominantly illiterate, the play became a means of education. Sometimes the plays depicted important events in Spanish history like the battle between the Christians and the Moors.

Physical exercise was encouraged but not at the cost of sin. As late as April 26, 1877, the attorney general, in support of the Church's wishes, proclaimed that all persons engaging in playing baseball on Sunday were guilty of a violation of the "Sunday Law." These people were liable to prosecution and punishment.

20

Statehood for New Mexico

From the time New Mexico attained its status as a US Territory, it began to petition for statehood. Between 1849 and 1910, fifty acts were introduced for statehood. Just as quickly, New Mexico was denied these requests. At first, the reason was the slavery issue, later it was because of the antagonism over Reconstruction. Perhaps greater than these excuses were these two: religious bigotry and racial discrimination. Anglo-Americans did not really accept that New Mexico was a part of the United States. After all, they reasoned, the language was not English; the culture was foreign; and the Catholic Church was all-powerful. Behind the scenes were those New Mexicans who did not want statehood but would not speak out against it. These were the great landowners and large merchants who were afraid they would have to pay much higher taxes as part of the Union.

Between December 1891 and June 1903, no fewer than 20 bills were introduced to admit New Mexico to statehood. Only three passed the House and then died. Easterners were afraid the West would become too powerful and they also feared having more pro-silver clout in the Senate.

In a peculiar way, the Spanish-American War did some good for the cause of statehood. More of Theodore Roosevelt's Rough Riders came from New Mexico and Arizona than any other area. After the war, Theodore Roosevelt kept in touch with many of his Rough Riders. The first reunion was held in Las Vegas, New Mexico in June 1899.

While there Roosevelt pledged himself for statehood, saying: "All I shall say is if New Mexico wants to be a state, you can count me in, and I will go back to Washington to speak for you or do anything you wish."

On his way out to the West Coast, President McKinley was assassinated while stopping at Deming, New Mexico in May 1901. The leader of the Rough Riders, then Vice-President became President of the United States. To the disappointment of the people of the state, President Theodore Roosevelt did not follow through on his promise.

Because statehood for New Mexico had been so elusive a goal, the next step was to attempt to bring New Mexico and Arizona in jointly as one state. This proposal would clearly satisfy some of the easterners who feared too much power was being accumulated in the west. In the spring of 1902, it looked like it would be jointure or nothing. Most of the folks from Arizona were against this proposal. They argued that the people of the two territories were quite different. New Mexicans had a strong Mexican background while this was not true of Arizona. Besides, Arizona was reluctant to put its considerable mining interests under the control of Santa Fe. New Mexico favored jointure. A bill came to a vote for jointure but was defeated.

It was not until 1912 that New Mexico entered the Union as the forty-seventh state followed by Arizona, the same year, as the forty-eighth state. More than a century of national expansion culminated on February 14, 1912 when President William Howard Taft signed the long-awaited proclamation. This was also the year that Alaska was granted territorial status in the United States.

Four centuries in review show us that Santa Fe is anything but an ordinary city and likewise New Mexico is anything but an ordinary state. In the years that followed the proclamation of statehood, the people of New Mexico began more and more to integrate themselves with the rest of the nation. Growing pains were evident but the West was open for business. No longer were the Indians creating problems for the inhabitants (though we may have a different view of the struggle today than we did in the time of Kit Carson). No longer did France, Spain or Mexico lay claim to the Southwest (although Pancho Villa raided Columbus, New Mexico in 1916). No longer did visitors come to Santa Fe expecting to see what they had left in their hometowns, the same kind of lifestyle or the same kind of Anglo building construction. Above all, no longer did the visitors want to see New Mexico copy what was taking place in the East.

A new and genuine appreciation grew for the ancient city. Even the "Styles Ordinance" had for its primary goal to recreate the look of adobe in the center of town. The tourist wanted to see what was old— the older the better. Although the American tourists still flock to Europe to see the old cathedrals and plazas, they have a certain pride in knowing that their own Santa Fe boasts a similar heritage.

Among the architects to come to Santa Fe from Colorado was Isaac H. Rapp. He had an innovative spirit and did not mind experimenting, although his attempt at creating a Santa Fe Style ended up looking more like California Revival. About the time the Old Palace was being remodeled by Nusbaum, Rapp built the Scottish Rite Temple, modeled after the famous gate of the Alhambra in Granada, Spain.

Artists came to Santa Fe for a multitude of reasons. In 1917, the Museum of Fine Arts was dedicated. That same year, Georgia O'Keeffe visited the state for the first time. Writers came for the freedom; painters came for the light; and tourists came for everything they could see or buy.

Some like John Gaw Meem came because of a respiratory illness and stayed to make a lasting impression on the architecture of the city.

During the Second World War, Los Alamos took its place on the international stage with the creation of the Manhattan Project. Invited to New Mexico to create the atomic bomb were some of the greatest minds in the world. Today, it would take a sleuth of exceptional ability to find the administrative office of the Manhattan Project among the antiques and flowers on Palace Avenue.

In 1957, The Santa Fe Opera opened and was called the "Miracle in the Desert." American Indian artists were encouraged with the establishment by Executive Order under President Kennedy in 1962 of the Institute of American Indian Arts (IAIA) formerly known under a much longer title.

Today, thousands of visitors come to Santa Fe for the music, the theatre, for the scores of galleries, for the Spanish and Indian Markets and for a sojourn into the past. In 1998, New Mexico celebrated its Cuartocentenario—four hundred years of existence. Those of us who call Santa Fe home are proud of what our city was in the past and what it has, over the years, become. And the visitors who are always among us, seem to be delighted by the city's history, its culture and its charm.

Printed in the United States
98298LV00005B/73-75/A